REASONS TO SUFFER

A Journey from Doubt to Faith Guided
by the 1st and 2nd Letters of Peter

JONATHAN D. HUTCHISON

For more information, email jdhutchison@jdh48.com

ISBN: 978-1-7366440-0-3 Paperback
ISBN: 978-1-7366440-1-0 eBook

Contents

Introduction to 1st and 2nd Peter

"For it is a credit to you if, being aware of God, you endure
pain while suffering unjustly. If you endure when you are
beaten for doing wrong, what credit is that? But if you endure
when you do right and suffer for it, you have God's approval."

1 Peter 2:19–20

THIS BOOK IS the result of a conversation I had with a friend of mine.
At the time, I was his pastor. He asked me, "Just what does the Bible
mean by suffering? Why would God let us suffer?"

My answer began with this definition: "Suffering is an act of giving up
something valued for the sake of something else regarded as more important
or worthy." This definition came from a dictionary, not some theological
resource. I figured we'd start there and move to the Bible a bit later.

My friend got the concept quickly, agreeing that suffering could end
up being an act of giving up one's life for something of greater value. This
is what folks such as soldiers, first responders, and folks working with
Covid-19 patients do. He understood their work involved making a sacrifice. Then from somewhere in his memory bank, he recalled reading in the
Bible that Jesus had sacrificed himself for the benefit of all humankind.
But that was Jesus. My friend figured he would never be asked to give up
his life as Jesus did.

I circled back to our working, non-Biblical definition and what my friend understood that to mean for him as a Christian. He asked, "But that kind of sacrifice would take a lot of faith and belief and trust, wouldn't it?"

And that's when I suggested we look at the 1st and 2nd Letters of St. Peter found in the New Testament of the Holy Bible for possible answers.

I share this anecdote so you understand that you are not alone in asking the question, *Why do I have to suffer?*

You and I know that suffering has been with us right from the time of Adam and Eve. We've been told suffering is the price we pay for how we live and conduct ourselves.

As we think about suffering, we know that some suffering is unavoidable. Our bodies slowly fail us. We can't play as hard as we once could, nor can we continue with our favorite physical pastimes.

Our minds become less sharp. We have trouble finding the words we need or recalling the names of our friends and family.

Our spirits have good days and bad. Some days you and I can accept the discomfort and limitations in our lives. On other days we may feel abandoned by family and friends, sensing a lack of faith and hope in our futures. This suffering of our Spirit may be the hardest form of suffering that we will be called upon to confront.

When you and I admit we have lost faith, hope, or a sense that we cannot completely control our lives, we have uncovered one possible reason for our suffering. For people of faith, this brings up all sorts of questions:

Why do I suffer?

Why does God let me suffer?

Why do good people like me suffer while others don't?

In this resource, I hope that you may uncover some of the answers to those questions as we read the two letters of the apostle Peter from the New Testament of the Holy Bible. Even if the Bible is not a place you usually go for inspiration and guidance for living, let me assure you that Peter's letters and account of his experience with suffering and his journey to find a reason for suffering is a good place to start our study.

Peter lived in a time of social and political unrest. In his era, religious and political leaders persecuted those who disagreed with them. Religious and political groups controlled the news and the responses to what was occurring. People who spoke out against the authorities were imprisoned, tortured, and put to death.

One of the central issues at the time Peter wrote his letters had to do with the ministry of Jesus Christ, a teacher and prophet, who claimed he was the Son of God. Jesus' ministry upset both religious and civil leaders as it threatened those leaders' power and authority. Followers of Jesus had great faith in what they knew of Jesus and were willing to speak out for their faith in Jesus' message. As time went on, because of constant harassment and persecution, folks began to doubt their faith in Jesus. And their willingness to stand up for what their faith demanded of them began to diminish.

Peter came to encourage followers of Jesus and reassure them that they would most definitely suffer at the hands of those in charge of the temple and the government. But he also said that in the end, they would find a reason and a reward for their suffering. Peter told his story of the suffering he had endured as he preached the message Jesus had taught him.

Peter discovered his central reason for the suffering he experienced—being led by the Holy Spirit to preach the Good News of Jesus Christ. He was able to keep on teaching and preaching because of his faith, a faith he had found on his journey of understanding. For Peter, all the trials and tribulations he had experienced while literally walking the road with Jesus gave him the strength to endure all the suffering and persecution in his present circumstances. Like Peter, our journeys of faith, walking alongside Jesus, can also strengthen us for the suffering we all experience in our lives.

One reason to endure suffering is the promise of blessing from God in this lifetime and the promise of eternal happiness and peace after our life on earth is completed. There is also another reason to endure suffering. As followers of Jesus who imitate his life in our lives, just as Jesus found joy and peace in doing His Father's will, we may also find that same joy and peace in our willingness to do God's will in our lives. This will require our sacrificing something we value for something even more valuable to others. This, as you recall, is our working definition of suffering.

Studying Suffering

Our Christian past deserves our study. The scriptures demand our attention. We are encouraged to engage in lively debate concerning passages of scripture that are difficult for you and me to understand. This faithful questioning and inquiry into our faith are among the many positive effects of small group studies. Together, small gatherings of believers can engage scripture and discover how those words point to the Holy Spirit's power to open minds and hearts to the gifts found in God's Word.

Whether you undertake this study as an individual or as a member of a small group, look to the scripture for the reasons why we should suffer for the Good News through joyful service. Let the scriptures guide you as you begin your journey of faith. Through your study, I hope you might discover a reason and a reward in your life to endure the suffering that affects us all in mind, body, and especially in our spirits. It begins with finding our faith, just as Peter did—a faith found in the Good News of Jesus Christ.

You are not the first person to question your faith in God as you interact with a world that increasingly provides believers like you with little support or affirmation. The fact you have picked up this resource might mean you haven't given up faith, and you are open to conversation and discovery related to living today as a faithful Christian in an increasingly complex world. We live in a world that is, in some ways, just as hostile to present-day Christians as the times when Peter and his followers first spoke to crowds longing for help.

You may be looking for a safe place to consider and test your understanding of scripture before venturing out and living in the knowledge, comfort, and counsel you have found in Christ and his teachings. This resource has been created to guide you on your faith journey.

Throughout this resource, you will be offered encouragement. I wrote this to support your journey as you ask questions and discover the power of faith through your reading and reflections on the 1st and 2nd Letters of Peter. By the end of your journey, I hope you'll discover the comfort and confidence to understand suffering, strengthening your faith to help you endure life's many challenges.

Peter's Message

Peter was a follower of Jesus Christ. He was one of the original twelve disciples Jesus selected to accompany him during his brief three-year ministry to the Jews and Gentiles. During the early days of organized religion, Peter's ministry centered around encouraging and challenging new converts and affirming those already struggling with questions of faith and the demands of following Jesus.

Peter sensed the anxiety of the times. He sought to assure those who heard him speak, calming those who were just beginning to confront their faith in Jesus Christ. In response to the anxiety and questioning, Peter preached hope. He offered early Christians encouragement as they struggled with the suffering caused by a world that was hostile to Christians.

Peter wrote his two letters to folks who relied on faithful lives and attitudes to comfort and protect them. His first letter served as a brief reminder of what Christians believed. It also confirmed that faithful believers meeting together in community would find comfort and assurance for living in times that forced even the most faithful believers to question the power and presence of Jesus in their lives.

Peter's second letter, whose authorship is in dispute, was a recognition that then, as is the case now, not all who speak on behalf of Jesus clearly understand and use the Gospel message for encouragement and assurance. There have always been "false" teachers and prophets who use the words of Jesus for their own purposes.

This second letter also was to call believers to work at their faith and understand what Peter sought to pass on to them. Both then and now, the value of strong faith was/is to provide comfort, understanding, assurance, and encouragement to folks experiencing all levels of suffering or the false teaching from those who caused others to doubt the Good News of Jesus.

How to Use This Resource

This resource is divided into eight sections—five dealing with the 1st Letter, and the remaining three sections addressing the 2nd Letter. There is also an epilogue with final comments about this journey.

Each section begins with a suggested reading of scripture. I have used the New Revised Standard Version of the Bible for my source quotations. If you are using another translation of the Bible, take notice of the similarities and differences in the words you will read. As you read the scriptures, you might want to keep a journal and jot down any words or phrases that seem unclear or raise questions. Then as you work through the remainder of each chapter, keep your journal accessible and continue to write down words and phrases to guide your thoughtful study.

Next, centering prayer is offered. Read each prayer slowly. Let your prayers permit you to begin a conversation with God. Take time at the end of each prayer to be still. Once again, write down any words or phrases that appear in your thoughts. You may be hearing the voice of the Holy Spirit guiding you during your study and prayer time.

Finally, various questions and statements are provided to help you identify the challenges and issues addressed by scripture. Specific verses of scripture may be highlighted for your consideration. Those same verses may also be used as conversation starters if this resource is used in a small group setting. As in the church's early days, scripture is meant to bring new understanding and new insight to those on their faith journeys.

A Final Word before Beginning

It's always good to know and trust in the things in which you believe. Faith is a constant testing of the truth of your beliefs, and the strength and confidence those words of encouragement provide you. Never doubt the value—either when questioning or discussing scripture—of the tremendous help others can offer you as you seek to understand and trust in scripture.

I used to end almost every sermon I preached with a question to my congregation: "Do you believe this?"

Your faith is meant to help you. Your faith journey may help clarify your beliefs and encourage you to find great hope in whatever situation you find yourself. Strive to find peace and confidence in your beliefs and your faith. Then, with that confidence, go out into the world. Gather with others who are also seeking comfort through the scriptures.

Simply put, what we believe affects our actions in life. Those actions lead to reactions from others concerning our activities. In turn, how we respond to others based on our beliefs may be an excellent witness to the power and promise found in Peter's two letters. Strengthen your beliefs, trust in them, and have faith in those beliefs. We are never alone as we acknowledge our doubts, and we are never alone as we seek to develop our faith. It may just be that the more comfortable you and I are in asking questions, the greater our ability will be to build on our faith.

As I did, I hope you will find your reason to embrace suffering, a reason for holding on to your faith and the promises found in these two letters.

Once again, I encourage you to consider keeping a journal as you read the scriptures. Write down your questions and concerns and note how you are feeling. How do Peter's words encourage you as you continue your journey of faith?

Finally, before we begin, let me remind you once more that I am using the New Revised Standard Version (NRSV) of these New Testament scriptures. While it may be easier to have the same translation when you read each assignment, any translation or version of the scriptures will do. In fact, comparing translations, especially the use of words, may help you in hearing the messages the scriptures offer.

This study guide is designed to encourage your dedication to following Christ and finding joy in suffering. Take these words to heart for your journey ahead: "Therefore I intend to keep on reminding you of these things, though you know them already and are established in the truth that has come to you." (2 Peter 1:12) Enjoy your study and your journey.

Chapter One

Five Recurring Themes in the Two Letters of Peter

A S YOU ARE reading these two letters, notice Peter has five key themes or messages he repeatedly offers his readers. It may help to write down these themes and refer to them often as you study the two letters. Keep asking yourself how what you are discovering relates to Peter's five themes. Although these themes correlate to some degree to their respective chapters, note that Peter intertwines his five themes throughout his two letters.

Theme One - Belief in Christ

"May grace and peace be yours in abundance in the knowledge of God and of Jesus our Lord."

2 Peter 1:2

It's sometimes confusing when you and I are asked to have faith in someone or something while at the same time having doubts about what we believe. As Christians, we are frequently challenged by our friends and even our pastors as to our understanding of scripture itself. It's difficult to have confidence in what we believe and what we are called to do as followers of Christ when we aren't completely sure of the correctness of what we understand scripture to say.

For instance, followers of Christ believe in life after death—a glorious life in heaven for those who have been faithful and obedient to the words of scripture. Our belief about an afterlife makes it possible for us here on earth to endure the challenges expected of us, all the while anticipating eternal life. Believing in a loving Creator God makes it easier to approach God in prayer, considering that God's love and mercy will guide God's response to us. God's love for us allows you and me to believe God will not harm or abandon us. This is a God who will be with us in our suffering, just as that same God was with Jesus in his suffering.

Peter challenges those who hear his words to trust those words. So, when hardship does come, as it always does to followers of Christ, our beliefs and our trust will sustain us, no matter what the challenges or suffering may be.

Knowing what you believe and having confidence in those beliefs can be a strong defense in times of anxiety, confusion, and suffering. You will encounter this first theme in Chapter Two of the study.

Theme Two - Suffering and Faith

"But even if you suffer for doing what is right, you are blessed.
Do not fear what they fear, and do not be intimidated."

1 Peter 3:14

Suffering for one's faith happens to all followers of Christ. It may be a mild form of suffering, such as being singled out for your faith or religious practice by members of your family, friends, or co-workers. Or suffering may produce a profound physical, emotional, or spiritual experience. Regardless of the severity of our suffering, those who openly profess faith in Jesus Christ will face some form of suffering and discrimination. This has always been the case.

In your experience, you may find that suffering in body and mind is easier to understand and fix than suffering in the Spirit. Spiritual suffering causes us to slowly begin to doubt ourselves, our faith, and our commitment to the vows we took as Christians. Spiritual suffering occurs because we doubt the promises and assurances that we have been taught will be our rewards for living a life following Jesus.

In his letters, Peter is quite clear about his suffering for the sake of his faith in Jesus. He is also clear that he gladly suffers for his faith, even as Jesus suffered for his faith. Peter returns to this theme time and time again. Based on the subject of this theme and many of our real-life experiences, it's clear Christians will suffer as a result of living out their beliefs. Part of being a Christian is to open yourself up to the questions and doubts of our families and friends who have chosen differing lifestyles and behaviors. This by itself may cause some level of anxiety and tension.

What is still unclear for many Christians, then and now, is if followers of Christ can find joy or purpose in their suffering. Peter offered reasons for us to seek joy and meaning in suffering for the sake of Jesus. He preached the Good News of Jesus Christ and the promises of God for encouragement.

When I joined the church at thirteen, my minister did not spend a lot of time discussing suffering as part of being a follower of Jesus. But the more I studied scripture and read about the life of the original disciples, I began to figure out that to follow Jesus meant I would eventually face suffering for my belief in him. The challenge for Christians is to find purpose in that suffering. In these two letters, Peter offers us a purpose for our suffering in the life and example of Jesus Christ. This second theme will clearly be discussed in Chapters Three and Six of the study guide.

Theme Three - Don't Be Discouraged or Misled

"But false prophets also arose among the people, just as there will be false teachers among you, who will secretly bring in destructive opinions ... And in their greed they will exploit you with deceptive words."

2 Peter 2:1,3

Peter cautioned his listeners to be on the watch for false prophets who offered a differing interpretation of scriptures than the lessons taught by Peter and his followers. False teachers attempted to convince Jesus' followers that they could still live as they always had. They emphasized that there was no need to give up worldly pleasures as a requirement to live in a society increasingly defined by Jesus' teachings. The scriptural interpretations of the false teachers were meant to tempt Jesus' followers toward unholy living. These false teachers also used scripture to build up followers who were inclined to accept such false teachers' promises and assurances.

In my lifetime, as I tried to make sense of my commitment to Jesus, I have heard and seen false teachers at work. Jim Jones and the tragedy of Guyana, Waco and David Koresh, and Heaven's Gate, a cult begun by a former minister from a mainline denomination. All these false teachers and their groups started out helping others, studying scriptures, and building community. By appealing to the doubts some Christians had in their experience with the world around them, these false teachers offered an inaccurate but believable interpretation of scripture. Scripture was used to justify all sorts of behaviors and attitudes: slavery, polygamy, and false claims about when the world would end.

Some false teachers have used their knowledge to sway opinion to their advantage. For instance, they have used scripture to subvert the role of women and children in the church, exclude some lifestyles from the church, and ostracize the conduct of Christians who have steadfastly attempted to follow Jesus' example. False teachers spread confusion and doubt. In contrast, teachers empowered by the Spirit guide others in living a life of service, adhering to the lessons found in the ministry and example of Jesus Christ.

Peter believed the Holy Spirit inspired and directed all true teachers and prophets. Those teachers who lived in the Spirit could be recognized by their actions and their relationships with those they ministered to. Learning how one recognized Spirit-led teachers as well as recognizing false teachers was the challenge new converts to Christ faced as they sought to live according to the Word of God. This third theme will be further discussed in Chapters Four and Five of your study.

Theme Four - Receive Power from God

"And after you have suffered for a little while, the God of all grace, who has called you to his eternal glory in Christ, will himself restore, support, strengthen and establish you."

1 Peter 5:10

Peter assured his followers that God would never abandon faithful and obedient followers of Christ. God watches over all believers and provides them with strength and determination to stand up to possible ridicule while advocating for a life of faith. God brings other believers together in various communities so that believers can affirm and nurture one another. One's faith journey is very personal, but it benefits from interaction, study, and discussion with other believers who are also on their own faith journeys. Christians should seek other Christians and come together to worship, pray, study, and nurture one another.

In God's love for all, God is continuously building up faithful followers who seek the truth found in the Gospel messages. God welcomes new lives into the church. God also welcomes those who embark on the lifelong journey of adherence to God's commands and living according to the example of Jesus.

Just as the Holy Spirit came upon followers of Jesus at Pentecost, transforming lives forever, so too, does the Holy Spirit continue to enter the lives of folks like you and me. God has given you and me free will to choose whether we will accept the power and the protection God holds out for each of us. This is the choice you and I make each day—whether we pursue holy or unholy living.

Peter was convinced that Christ's followers were called to a life in Christ, guided by the Holy Spirit, and affirmed by actions and beliefs that agreed with the teachings of Jesus. Once again, Peter stressed the importance of gathering in a community of believers who continuously reminded one another of God's power and the power of the Gospel message to transform lives and make disciples of Jesus Christ.

In the words of another true prophet, St. Paul:

> And not only that, but we also boast in our sufferings, know-
> ing that suffering produces endurance and endurance produces
> character, and character produces hope, and hope does not
> disappoint us, because God's love has been poured into our
> hearts through the Holy Spirit that has been given to us.
>
> Romans 5:3–5

Let me offer you a quick suggestion. As you continue to study the Bible, compare the teachings of the four Gospels, the writings of Paul, Peter, and the other prophets whose teachings are found in the New Testament. Read how they agree on the fundamental issues for building up one's faith despite differences in cultural points of view and diverse audiences.

The fourth theme will be discussed in greater detail in Chapters Five, Six, Seven, and Eight.

Theme Five - Our Joy and Reward

> "Therefore prepare your minds for action; discipline your-
> selves; set all your hope on the grace that Jesus Christ will
> bring you when he is revealed."
>
> 1 Peter 1:13

There is joy in living a life defined by the teachings of Christ, the power of the Holy Spirit, and the love of God who created all beings. According to Peter, joy is immediate in this life and has eternal consequences for believers when their lives here on earth are complete. Peter found joy in most everything—joy in preaching and teaching, joy in suffering, joy in working on his salvation and understanding, and joy in his relationships with the folks in the churches he inspired. Joy kept Peter going during all sorts of trials and times of doubt. Look for joy in your journey as you search for reasons to suffer with a joyful heart deeply rooted in your obedience to Christ.

As Peter found and shared his joy, he inspired followers to do the same. Joy comes from faithful obedience to the Good News of Jesus Christ. Joy is a choice believers are free to accept in their lives. Despite all obstacles, following Jesus opens new possibilities for joyful living and inspires you and me to continue our journeys in faith.

Steadfast faithfulness, obedience, and a sincere choice to live as Christ lived all bring the rewards of redemption and salvation. Simply put, joy in Christ is one of the rewards believers receive as they follow their journey of faith and discovery. Joy, especially when found through your faith, is a reason to persevere when we are tempted away from Christ.

Theme five will be discussed in more detail in Chapters Two, Five, Six, and Nine in the study guide.

These five themes were important to Peter. They will also be important to you as you discover reasons for enduring suffering and reasons to find joy in challenging yourself to live in complete obedience to God, Christ, and the Holy Spirit. This is part of the sacrifice each Christian is called to make as unholy living gives way to a life of holy purpose.

As you read the scriptures, reflect on the questions and comments following each reading, and as you consider the questions at the end of each chapter, take time to review the message of the five themes. Once again, I encourage you to write down your thoughts and questions in your journal during times of personal reflection.

I hope that finding a reason for joy despite suffering is what this resource will help you discover. Feel comfortable with your questions and your concerns. You are not alone in working out the demands of a life following Christ's example. Remember Peter's encouragement assuring you that you already possess the necessary wisdom and perspective to confidently explore and discover the depth of your faith.

Chapter Two

Do You Believe This?

BEFORE READING THIS chapter, go to your Bible and read 1 Peter 1:1–25. Be sure to grab your journal and write down any questions from your reading of the Holy Bible or this chapter.

> Let's begin in prayer:
> Gracious God, as we begin this study concerning suffering for our beliefs, may we find comfort and encouragement in the words of your prophet, Peter. May we learn to have faith in his experience and understanding, and to take on the task for which he prepares us. Guide us to grow in our faith continually and steadfastly and in our willingness to do whatever is required to live as did your Son, Jesus. When we are anxious, give us calm; when we are at war with ourselves and those with whom we live and worship, help us find peace; when we are suffering, show us the purpose in our struggles. We await a new understanding and a new belief. In Jesus' name. Amen.

When I was about four years old, my father joined the US Army as a chaplain. Wherever my father was, he would send me letters every so often from the places he was stationed. I received letters from Korea, Germany, Japan, and various Army posts in the US. The letters from my father ended about the time I graduated from college. However, for about seventeen or eighteen years, those letters taught me about people and places beyond my imagination. I had faith in my father's reporting and grew to believe all that he said. When I could verify my father's narrative with facts that confirmed what I had read in those letters, my confidence in my father and his words grew.

Whenever I received a letter from my father, I would immediately find a map of where he was stationed. I learned about new countries, people, and experiences, all from those occasional letters. I read about places, people, and adventures for which I had no foundational understanding. But over time, as each letter arrived, I challenged myself to learn all I could from the content of those letters. I began to believe things by faith; I had faith in my father's messages, and my faith was confirmed by my digging into the *World Book Encyclopedia*, *National Geographic* magazines, and any other supporting information I could find. I got to know my father and trust what he wrote through his letters and photographs.

Similarly, the people who heard Peter's letters became aware of his experience of knowing Jesus, and of his growing trust in the faith he found in Jesus' words and actions. Peter shared the story of his suffering, his persecution, and the danger all around him. His message was clear—his faith protected him and gave him the strength and confidence he relied upon as he spread the Good News of Jesus, even as others tried to silence him. In Jesus' ministry, Peter had found a reason to endure the suffering he experienced.

Just as I sought other resources to confirm the content of my father's letters, I invite you to dive into any references that may help you understand and explore your faith in the Good News Peter offered his followers. In addition to this guide, a good study Bible might be a great resource to have available as you read and review Peter's two letters. Each different translation of the Holy Bible usually has its own study Bible available, either online, at the library, or at a bookstore.

Discovering What We Believe In

The 1st letter from Peter to the exiles (a term used to identify Jews returning to their homes after their captivity) is an attempt to encourage those in remote places to gather as those chosen and destined by God to pledge their lives to Jesus Christ. (See 1 Peter 1:1–2) How did folks respond to hearing they had been chosen and destined by God to follow the example of Jesus' teachings?

After hearing God's Word and learning to worship Jesus, many were led to be baptized by water and the Holy Spirit. In baptism, people confessed their belief in Jesus and pledged their faith and trust in him. They surrendered their lives to Jesus to be part of Jesus' saving grace and heirs to Jesus' promises. Peter knew that being baptized and being identified as a follower of Christ would not be easy in this time of persecution and general mistreatment of new converts. And that is why Peter shared the story of his life at the hands of religious and civil leaders who sought to put a stop to his teaching. In 1 Peter 1:2, Peter prayed that abundant grace and peace would comfort and protect newly baptized followers of Jesus.

Peter wasted no time in addressing the issue of suffering for one's faith. In 1 Peter 1:3 we read, "… by his great mercy he has given us a new birth into a living hope …" Peter's message stressed that persistent faith would be needed to stand up to the challenges of being a follower of Christ. And this faith did not come without a cost. The cost was suffering for one's faith and one's salvation. Peter encouraged his listeners to persevere, and as you and I read in 1 Peter 1:6:

> In this you rejoice, even if now for a little while you have had to suffer various trials, so that the genuineness of your faith … may be found to result in praise and glory and honor when Jesus Christ is revealed.

All change requires some degree of suffering. Those early Christians sacrificed their safety, their livelihood, and in fact their very freedom, for their belief in Jesus Christ and the promises of salvation and eternal life that Jesus offered. The people trusted in prophets such as Peter, and his recounting of how he came to believe and trust in all that he knew and had learned at Jesus' side.

Peter's life was forever changed by what he heard and trusted in—the words and ministry of Jesus Christ. And for that decision to follow Jesus, Peter suffered at the hands of religious and civil leaders. But his suffering resulted in his finding joy in the knowledge that Jesus Christ would lead him to salvation and eternal life. After being in the presence of Jesus, Peter realized that he and those to whom he preached could find "indescribable and glorious joy" even though that joy would carry the almost certain price of suffering and persecution.

To sacrifice, to suffer, to believe in things unknown and unseen takes preparation and commitment. It is a path strengthened by discipline and obedience. As the scripture teaches in 1 Peter 1:13–15:

> Therefore prepare your minds for action, discipline yourselves; set all your hope on the grace that Jesus Christ will bring you when he is revealed. Like obedient children, do not be conformed to the desires that you formerly had in ignorance. Instead, as he who called you is holy, be holy yourselves in all your conduct …

Although Peter had once been a fisherman, he was also called to be a prophet. Peter had previously conformed to the religious and civil laws and customs of his time. Now Peter lived by new religious and civil laws and customs, learned as he followed Jesus, trusting in the Good News Jesus had taught him. Peter's surrender to this new way of living, these new rules and customs put him in peril of persecution. Yet he went on in joy and the certainty that any suffering he endured for the truth found in Jesus Christ was indeed a price he was willing to pay.

We read in 1 Peter 1:21: "Through him you have come to trust in God, who raised him from the dead and gave him glory so that your faith and hope are set on God." Peter also offered these words (in 1 Peter 1:22): "Now that you have purified your souls by your obedience to the truth so that you have genuine mutual love, love one another deeply from the heart." Surrendering to Jesus included freely taking on a new life of service. Surrender involved pledging yourself to a new way of life, a new purpose, leaving behind the old and corrupt practices for a new and holy way of living.

Peter was one of a small group of Jesus' disciples. Those disciples tested each other; they debated each other; they learned from each other, and they trusted each other. They were a small group, a community of like-minded believers of radically new ideas, especially the Good News of Jesus Christ. And for that, they would suffer and be persecuted by religious and civil authorities.

Jesus first called his disciples, and Peter then called his followers to joy, to obedience, and to an intentional new way of living. This way rested on faith in Jesus' words and surrender to hope which led to salvation and new life. In the early Christian Church, living a Christlike life would end in pain and sacrifice for many followers of Jesus' teaching. But Peter's example, Jesus' ministry, and growing trust and obedience to a new way of living and loving compelled new converts to leave the old ways behind. Peter called these new believers to conform to an alternative standard—a standard of truth, love, and mutual effort to endure suffering and to spread the Good News of Jesus Christ.

Further Consideration and Action

If you are using this resource for individual study, consider adding to the journal you have already begun by noting any questions, thoughts, or concerns that arose while reading this chapter. Then as you encounter the questions and comments suggested below, think how this chapter has helped you explore just what you believe as a follower of Christ. Where do you sense opportunities to grow in your faith and understanding?

If you are using this resource in a small study group setting, share your questions and concerns with the other group members. See what questions and comments the group has in common. How can you help each other discover a new understanding of the scriptures and the guidance those scriptures offer?

The crowds believed Peter because he was one of the original disciples. He was with Jesus every day for three years. Peter was the Rock upon which Jesus' church would grow. Peter suffered for his faith, but he never gave up his belief in Jesus.

- Why did people who first heard Peter speak trust and believe in his teaching?
- If you had heard Peter speak or invite you to become a follower of Jesus, what would have convinced you to trust in Peter's words?

The church continued to grow even after Peter died. In fact, it continued to grow rapidly for hundreds of years. This growth came about even though Jesus or Peter was not around to lead or teach potential new converts.

- On what basis did people believe those who preached the Good News?
- Why were people willing to suffer for this faith, believing in things they hadn't experienced firsthand?
- Who do you trust to preach and teach the Good News to you and those you love?
- What makes them believable and trustworthy to you?

Remember back to Pentecost when Jesus told the original disciples to wait until the Holy Spirit came upon them to equip them for ministry in Jesus' name? Consider the following:

- What function did the Holy Spirit have in assisting folks to believe in the Good News?
- Would the early church have continued to grow without the Holy Spirit at work?
- How have you experienced the Holy Spirit at work in you? In others?

Followers of Christ were willing to suffer, be persecuted, and even give their lives in obedience to the words they read in scripture. They believed in transforming their lives, guided by the Spirit to obey and trust in Jesus.

- For what would you be willing to suffer? For what would you be ready to die?
- Is your faith and belief in Jesus one of the things for which you would willingly suffer and perhaps even die for? Why or why not?

One of the early Christian Church's strengths was a sense of community—one where everyone gathered in hearing of, obeying, and living out a life directed by the Word of God and the Good News of Jesus Christ.

- With whom do you share your faith?
- Who helps you strengthen your faith and your understanding of what it means to suffer for "a little while until the genuineness of your faith" is shared?
- How might this affect the time you spend in worship, prayer, and study?
- In 1 Peter 1:15, Peter calls believers to be holy, to live holy lives. What makes a "holy life"?

And in 1 Peter 1:22, followers of Christ, aided by the Holy Spirit, are given instructions: "Now that you have purified your souls by your obedience to the truth so that you might have genuine mutual love, love one another deeply from the heart."

- What would a community of believers look like who were willing to sacrifice and suffer in obedience to this scripture? To scripture in general?

The challenge is to find such a place, such a group of people in whom you can confide as you grow your faith. Surround yourself with folks you trust who are confident in their faith.

- As you listen to these folks, ask yourself, what convinces you that they believe in what they say?
- What convinces you that you believe what you say and do as a follower of Jesus Christ?

Chapter Three

Act Like a Christian

BEFORE BEGINNING THIS chapter, grab your Bible and your journal and read 1 Peter 2:1–25. Keep in mind being a follower of Jesus is not just believing, but also acting as one who follows the example of Jesus in thought, word, and deed. That's what makes Peter's teaching and life experience such a powerful witness to those who heard him preach and teach.

> Now, let's begin in prayer:
> Creator of all, we come back to scripture to read your words, to be immersed in your hopes for us. Help us when we are distracted. Keep us safe when we wander. Bring us home to the company of believers. Help us to understand and follow the example of your Son, Jesus Christ. As we confront suffering for your sake and the sake of the Good News, strengthen our resolve to be good role models in a world wondering what Christ offers. We ask this in Christ's name. Amen.

About two months into my third-grade year, my parents told my sister and me that we were moving across town to a new house. That move also meant we would be attending a new school. Since my new school was small, everyone already knew one another, and after two months of being together, my new-to-me third-grade class in which I had been placed had already organized itself. The popular kids had already set the rules for everyone else—you were either in or out. Being a new arrival from across town, I had no place in the established social groups. I was an outsider, or at least that's how I felt. I believed I didn't fit in.

First came the bullies. They had their way with me. Then came the athletic types who declared that no one would ever choose me for their team. I had been banished into insignificance—just another new kid to neglect. Being a stranger in a new place was not going to be easy.

I decided the action for me to take was to imitate the popular kids. I became a keen observer of group dynamics and personality traits. I chose to fit in, to be just like everyone else. I figured this was my way to survive and remain unnoticed.

In high school, I decided to change my strategy. I decided to do the things that brought me joy, such as writing and painting and competing in long-distance races. Because these things brought me great pleasure and joy, I didn't mind all the extra time and sacrifice needed to improve my skills and performance. My persistent efforts resulted in recognition from teachers, coaches, and finally, my peers. People were noticing me. They asked my opinion. They listened to what I had to say.

While I was becoming confident in what I shared with folks at school, I was also quietly developing my faith in God. I attended church regularly. I sang in the choir, taught Sunday School to younger kids, and caught the eye of several adults who encouraged my faith journey. Many of the adults with whom I had contact in church welcomed my questions of faith. They spent countless hours with me, explaining the power and promise of hope. They encouraged me to accept Jesus into my life. Eventually, I joined the church and promised my faithful obedience to Jesus. I pledged to follow Jesus' example of how to live and how to treat others.

Like many who attended college in the late sixties, there were many distractions to keep me from imitating Christ in my thoughts and actions. I succumbed to the distractions. No one wanted to be around a Jesus freak. At that time, at my college, to openly admit belief in Jesus was to suffer ridicule from folks who were happy to lead me astray. I was not strong, and I was not faithful. I did not want to suffer for Jesus. Once again, I just wanted to blend in and disappear along with the crowd.

I graduated from college, unsure of who I was and who I wanted to be. I was not a faithful follower of Jesus, and I was not the rebel I'd chosen to imitate in college. I was adrift. I had no convictions other than those that brought me short-term periods of naive happiness. I lived for myself. I felt utterly alone, even when surrounded by lots of folks. I was miserable. I wasn't acting like a Christian.

As you read the commentary that follows, remember how in the story I just shared, I wanted to belong to some group of my peers. I was tempted to adopt new behaviors, new beliefs, and new friends just to be accepted. If that meant straying from the example of Jesus as preached by Peter and found in scripture, I was willing to consider that action. But then, I wouldn't be living nor acting as a true follower of Christ would. That's what people would see in me. They would have no reason to trust what I said or did as being representative of the teachings of Jesus.

Conforming to This World

In the early church, around the end of the first century, many folks were hearing about Jesus for the first time. Jews and non-Jews (the Gentiles) were openly debating the faith taught to them by rabbis and other religious teachers. These same people would end up wrestling with a life imitating their newfound savior, Jesus, of whom Peter now spoke.

During those early years after Jesus' death, folks had to decide to live either by the example of Jesus, the dominant civil leaders' standards, or the teaching of various false prophets who promised that Jews and Gentiles could maintain their present standard of reckless living. Those false prophets taught that one could follow Jesus and civil authorities and still eat, drink, and be merry just as people had always done. The message of the new teachers was tempting. According to these false teachers, in one's life, there was no need for sacrifice or suffering. One did not have to follow Jesus to be acceptable in the eyes of those false teachers.

In the second chapter of Peter's first letter to his churches, he offered his guidance to all those who would listen. Peter described what it meant to be part of God's people. He laid out what a life following Jesus would entail. He prophesied and preached the price for a life reflecting Jesus Christ's example. In 1 Peter 2:1–3, we read:

> Rid yourselves, therefore, of all malice, and all guile, insincerity, envy, and all slander. Like newborn infants, long for the pure, spiritual milk, so that by it you may grow into salvation—if indeed you have tasted that the Lord is good.

I always wondered why Peter chose those particular behaviors as the indicators of improper living for a follower of Jesus Christ. Were those the most general behavioral characteristics of both Jews and Gentiles at the time of Peter's ministry? Imagine treating another person with malice or insincerity, or slanderous remarks. Those behaviors didn't do much to foster friendship and community. Indeed, those attitudes would tend to weaken the bonds of a group whose members depended on one another. A strong bond was crucial as this group was breaking away from the power and authority of the prevailing religious and civil societal norms.

And that was not the kind of life that Jesus and Peter lived and taught. Peter's experience with Jesus had transformed him. A simple fisherman, Peter had been tasked with and accepted the call of Jesus to present a new way of living, a new basis for community, and faithful obedience to scriptural demands. Peter was also clear that people under his care were just beginning to figure out their relationship with Christ. That's why communities of believers were so crucial (then and now) for faith formation and ongoing education and study. You and I are invited to be fed on nourishment provided in God's Word, and that's more effective and satisfying when done together.

After considering new attitudes and behaviors based on the Good News of Jesus Christ, new converts to the Way of Jesus would find the courage and faith to obey the scriptures and live a life worthy of salvation and worthy of imitation by other new believers. They might even find a reason to endure and accept suffering for the Good News and their faith.

In the first few years after Jesus' death and at the time Peter was writing his letters, Jesus was still an unknown entity to many who had never heard him preach or seen him heal or watched him perform miracles. But once folks heard the words of prophets like Peter and became open to the Holy Spirit guiding their lives, once they believed, they experienced just how powerful and life-changing faith in Jesus could be. To non-believers, Jesus was a troublemaker and a rebel, contradicting leaders of the Jewish faith. He was also an irritant to Roman civil leadership. But to believers, Jesus offered hope and new beginnings.

Faithful followers developed confidence in their newfound beliefs. They began to act with a sense of new purpose, imitating the life of Christ, and it was a life transformed by new expectations and new standards. These behaviors and attitudes were the mark of a person who had chosen to live a holy life. Those who chose not to believe in the power of Jesus were instead influenced and controlled by the overwhelming vengeance and brutal authority of those who sought to halt the spread of the Good News preached by Peter.

Yet Peter persevered. He encouraged new converts and called them to fully accept life as a follower of Jesus. In 1 Peter 2:9, you and I can read:

> But you are a chosen race, a royal priesthood, a holy nation,
> God's own people, in order that you may proclaim the mighty
> acts of him who called you out of darkness into his mar-
> velous light.

At that time, folks would have been confused by those words, being identified as a holy people, a royal priesthood, God's people. All their lives, they had been treated poorly by their leaders. But Peter knew from his own experience of following his faith in Jesus that life in Christ was quite different. In the eyes of Jesus, people had immense value and great potential for goodness. In Jesus, all people had great worth. All were brothers and sisters of the same father.

Many people of faith were called to become leaders and priests for other new converts, and for those searching for meaning and purpose. Instead of living in despair and suffering at the hands of demanding and soulless leaders, new followers of Jesus were taught they could transform their families and friends' lives to accomplish noble purposes, of which the most basic noble purpose was following Christ.

Through faith in Jesus, God offered salvation, mercy, and protection. There would be, however, a price to be paid for these gifts from God. That price would be Jesus' death on the cross and his resurrection and ascension to heaven. And in turn, the price people paid would be to suffer for "righteousness' sake." That meant that just as Jesus was tortured and died for his teaching, anyone following Jesus would also suffer and perhaps die for their belief in Christ and his message.

Jesus' sacrifice for others pointed his followers toward a new path they would have to travel. This path would lead his followers to find new meaning and hope in their lives—to bring light into the darkness. New friendships, new supportive communities of believers, new customs, and a new social order became the reality for Jesus' followers. They came to believe that they now lived under the protection of God's mercy and guidance. Peter concluded in 1 Peter 2:10: "Once you were not a people, but now you are God's people; once you had not received mercy, but now you have received mercy."

Peter understood new converts might be distracted and tempted to return to the more familiar customs and laws under which they had previously lived. He taught: "Conduct yourselves honorably among the Gentiles, so that, though they malign you as evildoers, they may see your honorable deeds and glorify God when he comes to judge." (1 Peter 2:12) You and I know the real test of one's faith is how one acts in the typical day-to-day exchanges between folks. Peter directed new converts to act in ways that pointed others toward what a life following Jesus looked like.

Living as strangers in a new land and being confronted with laws and customs unfamiliar to them was a challenge for those who took on the demands of following Christ. They were encouraged by Peter to obey the words of scripture, to trust in God's protection, and to be humble and obedient in the face of Jesus' sacrifice on the cross.

Even as they tried to live out the lessons taught to them, recent converts were threatened and harassed for their new and unfamiliar behaviors and attitudes. Civil and religious authorities, without mercy, persecuted followers of Jesus for their beliefs. To follow Peter's teaching and to accept the Good

News found in scripture was not something that could be approached with a casual attitude. A new life in Christ tested the limits of a new faith and the strength of one's character. Living as a Christian required a steadfast belief in the hope of eternal life and salvation supported by an unshakable faith in Christ. Suffering for one's faith was to be embraced and endured as a mark of a holy and righteous life. Faithful followers' willingness to surrender everything to Jesus would be a powerful witness to those who might be considering accepting Jesus.

All the while and despite the challenges, Peter encouraged those who heard his words to conduct themselves honorably. While encouraging others to adopt the teaching of Christ, right living would go a long way in convincing unbelievers to give up their old ways.

In 1 Peter 2:17, we read, "Honor everyone. Love the family of believers. Fear God. Honor the emperor." When challenged, you will remember that Jesus urged his followers to give to the emperor (civil authorities) what was due to the emperor and to give to God what was due to God. The challenging part of living as a follower of Jesus was and is still to live by Christ's example all the while living in a world often governed and defined by civil and religious leaders who have values that are counter to the teachings of Christ.

In recent times for instance, when prayer was abolished in schools, Christians first disagreed with that decision. Then, as a compromise, they reluctantly agreed to allow time for all students of any faith to have a time of meditation. Civil authority had effectively removed prayer from schools. Many influential religious leaders shied away from the conversation about school prayer, refusing to take a stand. They shied away from any conflict that might harm their image.

Contemporary society also debates topics like the death penalty or abortion, many times allowing civil authorities the final word on these ethical and moral decisions. Once again, many religious leaders turn away from standing up and speaking for the life-affirming example of Jesus. Many times, those religious leaders do not want to endure any negative response from being identified with a point of view not in alignment with contemporary societal norms.

Living as a Christian means having to take positions and support causes that are not popular or acceptable to many folks. It's standing as a witness for the values and beliefs Christians agree to when they accept Jesus into their lives. As a result, Christians suffer, sometimes sacrificing their comfort and safety for their beliefs.

Serving Two Worlds

Christians around the world are still persecuted and martyred for their faith. Yet, Christians are encouraged to not shrink from the requirements of following Jesus. In 1 Peter 2:13–14, we read:

> For the Lord's sake accept the authority of every human insti-
> tution, whether of the emperor as supreme, or of governors,
> as sent by him to punish those who do wrong and to praise
> those who do right.

Our freedom is found not by disobeying civil authority but in obeying God's will as offered to us in the example and ministry of Jesus. It is possible to be of this world but not conformed to this world. This manner of living is a challenge to one's faith and one's relationships with other people. We are all servants of one or more masters. We must choose who we will follow and, in turn, freely accept the ultimate rewards and penalties for our choices.

It is also true you and I are both masters to some and servants to some. We are responsible for our families and relationships. People under our care look to us for guidance and direction. They see us as their "masters." These are the folks for whom we are responsible.

Similarly, we are servants of the corporations for which we work. We are servants to the laws made for our protection. We are servants of the "greater good" that binds all people in unity. We are all accountable to someone in this world and to the God who has given us life. We serve both worlds—the civil world and religious, the temporal and eternal world. We are servants in both worlds. We are masters in the places and circumstances where we are called to lead and direct. We control the behaviors of some. The directives of others govern and control us.

Because we know how we as Christians are to treat others, we strive to love all, affirm and nurture those in our care, and bring the Good News of Jesus to those without the hope of salvation and eternal life. This task is one of our noble purposes in life. Put another way, we are to feed the hungry, give drink to the thirsty, clothe the naked, and visit those who are in any way separated from us. We are to serve God by attending to the least, the last, and the lost. In all of this, we are expected to act out of kindness and compassion for those known to us, as well as those unknown to us, those we serve, and those for whom we are responsible.

Unfortunately, the example of Jesus does not guide all masters. Masters can be harsh and brutal in their demands and their responses to the way of life of followers of Christ. We may find ourselves employed by an unjust or unkind master some time in our lives. We may suffer because of the attitudes and behaviors, even the abuse of our masters. Peter offered this teaching in 1 Peter 2:19–20.

> For it is a credit to you if, being aware of God, you endure pain while suffering unjustly. If you endure when you are beaten for doing wrong, what credit is that? But if you endure when you do right and suffer for it, you have God's approval.

If we are obedient to God and Jesus when we are in the position of being someone's master, it should be our intention never to cause people to suffer at our hands. Forcing others to suffer is not the way we follow God's direction. For followers of Christ, there is no reason for us to cause others to suffer.

Being a follower of Christ has its cost, just as it cost Jesus his life at the hands of those who wanted him destroyed. Jesus willingly found a purpose in his suffering—that we might be free to choose how we will live in this world. Will we follow Jesus, the good shepherd? This choice of who to follow is one of the challenges you and I have before us as it says in 1 Peter 2:25: "For you were going astray like sheep, but now you have returned to the shepherd and guardian of your souls."

There is an old hymn of the church, "Faith of Our Fathers," that reminds us of the level of faith we might aspire to. The first verse offers us these words:

Faith of our Fathers, living still, in spite of dungeon, fire, and sword; O how our hearts beat high with joy when'er we hear that glorious Word! Faith of our Fathers, holy faith! We will be true to thee till death.

It should be noted that in some hymnals, the first line of the verse reads, "Faith of the martyrs, living still" to emphasize that all Christians—men and women, young and old, past and present—are still potential martyrs or victims of the opinions and actions of those who seek to minimize the example of faithful Christians in the world.

We are called to surrender to Christ and sacrifice the easy pleasures and accomplishments of this life for the promises of salvation, freedom, and life in the world now and in times to come.

For Further Consideration and Action

Before you continue with the next section, stop and consider what you have just read. Faith guides our steadfastness in living like Jesus. One of our purposes is to offer an alternative way that leads to freedom and a new way of responding to the sometimes cruel and challenging world in which we live. We are exiles and aliens in a world that forces us to embrace a world that does not always offer us hope for eternity.

- What do you need to follow the Way of Jesus?
- What changes would you have to make in your life and your relationships to embrace the Way of Jesus?

It has been said that we live in a "between time," a time between the lessons taught by Jesus and the prophets and Jesus' coming again when He will gather faithful followers into a new heavenly kingdom. We are offered a choice. Because of the sacrifice and suffering of Jesus for our sake, followers of Jesus are free to choose how they will live out their faith.

- How can you and I prepare ourselves to choose the way of Christ, and how will we endure the suffering that will come?
- In what ways have you already experienced some degree of suffering for the practices and beliefs you have learned and accepted from your studying of the life and ministry of Jesus and Peter?
- How has that strengthened your faith and made you more willing and able to share your experience with others who may be suffering even now?

Surrounding ourselves with like-minded believers or even building our own supportive community can help us. Consider how you might join or enhance a supportive community.

- In what ways have you surrounded yourself with believers in Christ who have gone astray?
- In what ways have you surrounded yourself with others who have come back to the fold under the guidance of Jesus through the power of the Holy Spirit at work?
- How have you experienced the Holy Spirit actively working to assist you with the choices you make?

When we are united with Christ as members of his body, we join in his work of reconciling God's world with our world governed by religious and civil authority.

- What would you need to accept the call to step up to the next level of commitment and involvement to be part of a holy nation, one of God's people?
- What would it take for you to intentionally incorporate new Christlike behaviors in your life—behaviors and lifestyles most people do not necessarily value?

- Have you ever heard the phrase "becoming a disciple for Christ"? Do you know there are training programs to help folks take the next step toward committing to become actively involved in inviting others to grow their faith and commitment to Jesus? How might you discover these resources?

Gather together a small group of friends and discuss the issues Peter addressed in 1 Peter 2:

- living as an alien, an exile in a world hostile to Christians
- sacrificing the world we know for the world that Christ offers
- accepting the willingness to suffer for being identified as a follower of Christ
- identifying yourselves to others, as individuals and a small group, as those who belong to God.

Finally, consider your actions and behaviors and how they might be perceived by folks who are still reluctant to trust followers of Christ.

- What do people see and experience when watching your interactions with others, especially with others who are regularly overlooked by society?
- What is your responsibility to others for living in such a manner that brings credit and honor to behaviors and attitudes one might expect from a follower of Christ?
- By your actions or inactions, how are you directing folks to suffer or to be harmed because of their beliefs?

Chapter Four

Living as a Follower of Christ

BEFORE READING THIS chapter, grab your journal and turn to your Bible to read 1 Peter 3:1–22.

> Let us pray:
> Ever-loving God, you call us to a new way of living. You offer us guidance when we are struggling and reassurance when we suffer at the hands of those you have commanded us to love. Strengthen us for the trials we will face. When we suffer, guide our thoughts to gladly serving others. Help us amaze unbelievers with our steadfast faith in you, your Son, and the Holy Spirit. Lead us to new life. Remind us of the great gift Jesus offered us through his life, death, and resurrection. Give us confident faith to believe we can live as Christ instructed us. Through the words of your prophet Peter, teach us what will keep us in love with your way, through Jesus Christ, our Lord.

I have found there are times when living as a follower of Christ comes easily to me. And there are times when living as a follower of Christ seems impossible. Most times, when I go astray, something or someone leads me back to holy living. This brings me to two questions: *Can I always believe those who call me back? Am I willing to be called back?*

While I was in seminary, I served two small, rural churches as a student pastor. I was full of enthusiasm and boundless energy for ministry. Through my sermons and my ministry, I had high hopes that folks would flock to Jesus and surrender to living as Christ lived, serving others with a loving heart. I believed I would lead those under my care to great sacrificial living and a great desire to grasp a better way of living.

I wasn't at those churches long when one of the more senior church members approached me as I was getting into my car one morning after services. In a calm and gentle voice, she said, "Pastor, thank you for your ministry with us. But soon you will be graduating seminary and leaving us to get your first real church. As long as you are here with us, I would like you to do something for us."

I couldn't imagine what she was going to request of me, but I was ready for anything. Or so I thought. "Pastor, you seem very sincere about your faith. And while that is all well and good, we don't need to hear about your faith journey; we'd like you to listen to ours and help us by loving us and caring for us. We want to do better. Teach us the scriptures and let us hear the Good News. We are quick learners."

That's how our friendship began—with honesty and her reminding me that I was there to serve them, not to show them how wonderful and faithful I believed I was.

As I got to know this wonderful woman, I was inspired by her enthusiastic service to the church. I heard from other members of the things she did for the church and others in town who had no connection with our church. She visited shut-ins, prepared meals for families overwhelmed with life, and volunteered to drive folks to doctor appointments. Each week she dropped by to see those she had heard needed a bit of company. She was a true example of living her faith in very practical ways.

Through the grapevine, I also learned something else about this wonderful woman. She had been diagnosed with incurable cancer and had only months to live. Determined not to take pity on herself, she decided that her final days would be in service to the church and the people in her town. She was frequently in pain. Almost any activity was challenging, yet she never complained or let others know she was closing in on death. She served and suffered so others would have what they needed. She was peaceful despite her pain.

By the time she passed away, I had been appointed to another church. But I did go back for her funeral, where a former pastor officiated at her service. When he spoke, he said wonderful things about the woman. By her faithful service, she made it clear who was really in charge of teaching the people of that church about faith, service, sacrifice, living and suffering, and just loving others. The pastor said, "She was a faithful servant of Jesus, one who always served others, never complained, and never felt sorry for herself. She lived a life of faith inspired by what she had learned of Jesus from the scriptures."

Now, looking back at twenty years as a pastor, I still remember with great fondness the woman who set me straight. Some people do live as followers of Christ. Now in my retirement, I work to surround myself with faithful followers in my church and town. I live in greater hope because of that lovely woman and others who live as Christ commanded his followers to live.

Really Reading Scripture

As I reread the scriptures upon which this story is based (1 Peter 3:1–22), I realized the difficult challenges Peter's words created. Peter expected new converts to adopt a particular mindset and lifestyle, living as followers of Jesus Christ.

A casual reading of these verses does not suffice. Peter asked for minds to open, hearts to soften, and attitudes to change that would further good relations between Jews and Gentiles alike. These challenges uniting Christians and Jews ought to inspire followers of Christ, while at the same time assisting non-believers with their questions about faith and the lifestyle of those who follow Jesus.

Chapter 3:1–6 of Peter's first letter contains several themes, pointing to a central concept of improved interpersonal relationships. Many have read verse 3:1 and have been taught to see this verse as permission to condone women's subjugation. Let's reread verses 1 and 2:

> Wives, in the same way, accept the authority of your husbands, so that, even if some of them do not obey the word, they may be won over without a word by their wives' conduct, *when they see the purity and reverence of your lives.* (Italics added for emphasis)

The faithful woman I previously described in my story above, gifted me with a new understanding of what it is to live as a follower of Christ. Her faith was strong, even as mine was somewhat lacking. She had a great deal to teach me if I was willing to listen. In her, I saw the Holy Spirit at work, drawing others to join her in her care of the church, its members, and those she had yet to meet.

Here in these two verses, there is no suggestion that wives accept any authority or behavior that is abusive or hurtful. Staying in painful relationships was never the point of this instruction. Since it was difficult for women to be free of their husbands easily, women often endured more suffering than need be as they stayed true to their charge to care for the family. Experiencing his wife's care of her family, a husband might get a glimpse of the depth and strength of his wife's faith. Husbands had an opportunity to learn and grow in their self-awareness and their own faith by experiencing "the purity and reverence" in their wives' faithfulness to family, marriage, and duty.

Likewise, many Christians who are confused by some of the messages coming from the pulpit have been taught lessons out of context concerning verse three. This verse suggests women are instructed to refrain from adorning themselves outwardly with fine clothes and gold ornaments. Yet the meaning of this verse is made clear in 1 Peter 3:4, "rather, let your adornment be the inner self with the lasting beauty of a gentle and quiet spirit, which is very precious in God's sight." True beauty in a woman comes from within, a gentleness and a quiet Spirit that point to a safe and trusting place with which a wife can welcome, comfort, and nurture her family.

Since the theme of these verses is the duties and responsibilities of a husband and wife with and for one another, Peter next offers a lesson pointing to a good husband's duties.

> In 1 Peter 3:7, Peter taught:
> Husbands, in the same way, show consideration for your wives in your life together, paying honor to the woman as the weaker sex, since they too are also heirs of the gracious gift of life—so that nothing may hinder your prayers.

Scholars and many members of the clergy have debated the exact meaning of the phrase "weaker sex." The New International Version of the Bible translates this phrase as "the weaker *partner*" (italics added for emphasis). Whatever the intention, husbands are instructed to give honor to their wives. In homes where Christ is present, wives and husbands are expected to be partners. Having that understanding, husbands can go about their daily tasks and enter their prayer time with a heart free from thoughts that might limit or demean a wife's role and contribution to the marriage and the family. In a partnership, each person learns and grows because of and despite each partner's actions, behaviors, and faith. Each partner brings special gifts and talents to the relationship. Both the husband and wife each come to prayer and worship time to discover or discern one's misunderstandings and weaknesses, expecting to be strengthened and guided by conversations and insights with God.

It's essential to stop and consider a person's prayer time. Prayer is the most direct manner in which people can have conversations with God. Prayer time should be a time free from distraction, whether distractions of mind, body, or spirit. One comes to God in prayer to discover what can be changed in one's life. Prayer, in one sense, is a call for help. A husband cannot be open to developing better relationships with his wife if he is not open to his wife's great gift, or as Peter teaches, "the purity and reverence of their lives." In this letter, wives hear a special message of encouragement. They are affirmed they are unique creations of God, Abraham's daughters if they "do what is good and never let fears alarm" them.

In this scripture, wives hear they can absolutely influence their husbands by the depth of their faith and the purity and reverence of their lives. Wives can experience strength because of their faith, never letting fear force them into situations and attitudes that are harmful to them. Their faith is the foundation for their impact on the household. Here is an example of God's protective care for women of steadfast faith.

In response, husbands should be taught to value and affirm the obedient faith and inner strength of their wives. They ought to pray they will not do anything to impede their wife's actions taken on behalf of creating harmony within the household.

Recall the central theme of 1 Peter 3:1–7, creating and maintaining a good partnership in marriage. Each partner brings specific individual talents and gifts to a successful marriage and a faith-based home. More time and study should be spent on word choice or nuances of translation that define a husband as more in control of the family or suggesting that a wife is the weaker partner as many have been taught. However, those definitions do nothing to diminish each partner's obligation to work for the health and welfare of each other and their family. God will bring peace to each partner, and in that peace, prayers should be offered to God in thanksgiving for new insight. Husbands and wives should acknowledge the power of the Holy Spirit at work, leading each partner to offer compassion and love to one another through tender hearts and humble demeanor. Longing for more equitable roles should be the subject of prayers for partners and families.

The Christian Life Explained in Brief

In 1 Peter 3:8–22, Peter retells the hard lessons followers of Christ would face. Remember, developing one's faith is a lifelong journey of trial and error, instruction, and correction. There is value in gathering as a community of believers and surrounding oneself with a supportive group whose sole purpose is to commit to study and live as Christ requires of his followers.

The early church did not always help their community move toward Christ. Those first followers of Christ often divided folks into believers and non-believers, Jews and Gentiles. Some folks were embraced, and some were held in suspicious contempt. It is not surprising that leaders of current faith communities continue to divide people, using their authority and power to divide, harass, and persecute others just as surely as did the religious and civil leaders during the early church's formation.

Think of recent sermons you have heard or have read. Do they offer a path to peace and unity of purpose? Do they offer constant and steadfast instruction in living like Jesus in a world where Jesus is mentioned less and less? Do we only embrace current members' needs, or do we reach out to those beyond our walls, to folks who would benefit from hearing the Good News of Jesus Christ? Just how do we live as Christians, and what do we offer the world?

To answer these questions, Peter offers two lessons. The first lesson is introduced in 1 Peter 3:8–12, while the second lesson follows in 1 Peter 3:13–22.

In verse 12 of the third chapter, we read a summary of this section's theme: "For the eyes of the Lord are on the righteous, and his ears are open to their prayer. But the face of the Lord is against those who do evil." This verse speaks to the meaning of the word *righteous*. Living as followers of Christ certainly has an individual focus, meaning a benefit and challenge for each believer. But just as important to realize is that living as a follower of Christ includes how we, with our mutual understanding of Christ's example, treat others of our family in Christ. The relationship we forge with others is at the heart of what it means to be righteous. A righteous follower is morally good, or virtuous. A righteous follower is prepared to sacrifice and suffer for a greater good, goodness based on godly values.

Peter preached the behaviors of a righteous person. His words in verse eight were, "Finally, all of you, have unity of spirit, sympathy, love for one another, a tender heart, and a humble mind." In our relationships with followers of Christ, we are offered the choice of righteous, virtuous behaviors, or behaviors and attitudes that cause harm to others.

Those who observe followers of Christ from the sidelines gather much from the choices that believers make and the actions they take. Followers of Christ are called to "be a blessing" to others so that they will, in turn, receive blessings and encouragement from God. Living as a follower of Christ is to choose a more godly, righteous path day after day. God hears and answers our prayers, primarily if those prayers result in life-affirming, healing, helpful actions that benefit others.

What believers do as they interact with others can affirm the attitudes and behaviors potential converts experience as they decide whether to join a Christian community. Actions of those who call themselves Christians that demean others and are evil or intended to abuse will confuse those considering life as a follower of Christ.

An old hymn written in 1845 provides context for living as a follower of Christ. The first verse of that hymns reads:

> Once to every man and nation comes the moment to decide.
> In the strife of truth and falsehood, for the good or evil side;
> Some great cause, some great decision, off'ring each the bloom
> or blight, and the choice goes by forever 'twixt that darkness
> and that light.

This choice between good or evil is offered to those who would live as followers of Christ. As we shall see as we unpack Peter's second theme, found in 1 Peter 3:13–22, there is a price to be paid for the choices followers of Christ make, even when they choose the example of Christ. Christ sacrificed his life for the choices he made. There is no reason to believe present-day followers of Christ will not also face some level of suffering for the choices they make.

The result of Jesus' ministry and suffering would survive his death. His ministry would inspire diverse individuals to gather to live as Christ commanded. This was the life to which Peter was inviting those who heard his message.

One of the promises made to followers of Christ is in the end, Good (in other words, God) wins out, bringing light to the darkness and offering followers of Jesus protection and relief from persecution and suffering. Note Peter's words recorded in 1 Peter 3:13-14: "Now who will harm you if you are eager to do what is good? But even if you do suffer for doing what is right, you are blessed."

Present-day followers of Christ live in a time that will seldom require suffering for the message Christ offers. The term "convenient Christianity" is a phrase I used in my sermons to point out the limits of our willingness to suffer for the sake of the Gospel. Many Christians hold on to Christ until life following him gets messy.

We are fortunate in the United States that there are few instances resulting in adverse consequences occurring to those who are identified as being followers of Christ. In some parts of the world, those who choose to follow Christ do indeed suffer bodily persecution for their willingness to proclaim their faith in Jesus. In America, following Jesus is not the same threat to some religious and civil authorities as in places like the Middle East, North Korea, or China.

To the people who first heard Peter's words, they had to hide their faith. They met in secret so as not to be discovered or identified as followers of Christ. Their lives were always at risk as they attempted to live in a unity of Spirit, sympathy, and love for one another while maintaining a tender heart and a humble mind. Peter amplified that sentiment as he taught in 1 Peter 3:15b–16: "Always be ready to make your defense to anyone who demands from you an accounting for the hope that is in you; yet do it with gentleness and reverence."

In Peter's time, Christians quite literally suffered for their convictions. The threat to civil authorities was that Christians spoke of a new kingdom and a new king, and the civil authorities did not react well to potential challenges to their authority and power. We have read stories of the ancient church concerning how ruthlessly civil authorities treated anyone or any group that professed loyalty to Christ above civil authority. It was also true that religious leaders attacked Christ's early followers for the same perceived threats their civil counterparts imagined to be true.

Followers of Christ were asking inconvenient questions. They were upsetting societal standards and customs of that time. Such behaviors were a threat to the religious leaders' power, authority, and dominance. And so, followers of Christ suffered. In the face of their suffering, Peter offered encouragement to both Jews and Gentiles. "For it is better to suffer for doing good if suffering should be God's will, than suffering for doing evil." (1 Peter 3:18)

For Jesus' followers, suffering had its beginning in imitating the suffering Jesus endured as he went about his ministry among the least, the last, and the lost. Suffering was the response Christ's followers could expect as they came into more frequent conflict with civil and religious leaders who were frightened by this new religious movement.

Peter concluded this section and the theme of suffering with a mention of baptism's role in the lives of those who were learning how to live by the standards taught to believers by Christ and his disciples. We read in 1 Peter 3:21, "And baptism … now saves you—not as a removal of dirt from the body, but as an appeal to God for a good conscience, through the resurrection of Jesus Christ."

Salvation by faith and belief in Christ's suffering, death, resurrection, and ascension is confirmed and accepted by believers in the sacrament of baptism. In baptism, believers commit and vow to live following new standards of behavior. Believers pledge and promise to follow Christ's example and to intentionally imitate his path to a heavenly kingdom, all the while shedding the burdens of their present lives, trusting in God's protection and blessing. There is joy in living as Christ commanded.

Further Consideration and Action

As you think back about what you read in this chapter, take a moment to recall Peter's five themes. Peter seems to touch on three of the themes in this chapter: 1) Belief in Christ, 2) Suffering and Faith, and 3) Don't Be Discouraged or Misled. How might those themes affect your answers to the following questions?

Civil and religious leaders persecuted early followers of Christ because they feared losing what set them apart from those under their rule. Their self-proclaimed superiority was an attempt to intimidate those living under their authority.

- Who today attempts to take control of your faith by intimidation or persecution?
- What things cause you to suffer in mind, body, or spirit for your faith and living as a follower of Christ?

Baptism is a promise to renounce one's former life and to live and act in the ways Jesus taught his followers.

- If you have been baptized, what did you understand the Sacrament of Baptism to require of you?
- In what ways have you kept the promises you made at the time of your baptism?
- What would your life look like if you offered those with whom you have contact a unity of spirit, sympathy, love for one another, tender hearts, and a humble mind? What changes would that life require of you?
- How does the community of believers of which you are a part encourage you and others to share your gifts with others in your community, with others outside your group?

Acknowledging moral and ethical standards of a different era affects our understanding of the relationships we develop.

- How do you understand and respond to the challenges found in 1 Peter 3:1–7?
- What contributes to your present understanding of the roles and responsibilities of men and women in a relationship? Of your understanding of maintaining a family?

Consider the challenge of suffering for one's faith.

- In following the example of Jesus Christ, how is your suffering for your faith any more bearable or understandable?
- Do you believe that the "reward" for suffering for good brings God's blessing now and assures you eternal life in the future? Is that enough for you to bear the discomfort of being identified as a follower of Jesus Christ

In summary, consider these two questions:

- Consider the effect on potential new members when a Christian acts in a way that communicates "do as I say, not as I do," while we attempt to build up trust and invite new members to join our churches.
- How might this attitude lead to the hypocrisy that keeps folks from trusting the sincerity of many who call themselves followers of Christ?

Chapter Five

Encouragement Leading to Salvation

BEFORE READING THIS chapter grab your journal and your Bible and read 1 Peter 4:1–19.

> Let us pray:
> Father, you have offered us faith and strength to endure. You have reminded us of your love through the life and ministry of your Son, Jesus. Guide us now as we embrace salvation. Nurture us as we use the gifts and graces of new awareness as we live as an example of service and faith in your name. Help us believe any suffering that befalls us can be endured because of your promise of blessing to all those who suffer for spreading the Good News of Jesus. Give us the courage to invite others to come alongside us in following Jesus. We ask this in Jesus' name, our savior, and our hope. Amen.

In high school, I hung around with a kid I will call Tom. Tom was in a few classes with me, and since academics came more naturally to me than to Tom, I spent a lot of time helping him understand what we were supposed to be learning in class. It was not easy tutoring Tom; he got discouraged quickly.

Unlike my parents, Tom's parents never gave him any encouragement concerning his studies. They were always at him to spend less time studying and more time helping them with the family business. As time went on, any desire Tom had in succeeding at academic pursuits wavered. Eventually, he dropped out of school.

Tom's parents demanded much of his time. Over time his interest and involvement in the family business began to wane. And slowly, Tom drifted away from family and friends. He started hanging around with "a bad crowd." Push came to shove, and Tom ended up in the local jail. I heard the priest from Tom's church bailed him out. After his time in jail, his parents stopped caring altogether.

So at seventeen years old, Tom's life and his sense of hope came to a sudden stop. He saw no way forward but to fall in with a group of guys who spent all their time planning how to steal other people's possessions.

I tried to keep in touch with Tom. I wanted to offer him all the encouragement I could. Tom was slowly slipping into habits that probably would lead to disaster if left unchecked. This might have been the first time I really cared about one of the kids with whom I hung around.

I lost track of Tom as high school ended, and then I was off to college. When I was home from college, I'd go by his house from time to time, but he was never home. His parents, as I mentioned, had long stopped caring about his whereabouts. I'd ask around town about Tom, but no one seemed to have much information. All I could find out was that he was on the loose "doing something."

On one of my trips home from college, I was nearing home, driving through the center of town to get to my parent's house. I was lost in thought and not paying attention to my speed. Just as it dawned on me that I was speeding down the street, a police car pulled out, and lights began flashing. I pulled over, ready to be cited for speeding.

To my surprise, the policeman who approached my car turned out to be my old high school friend, Tom. I'm not sure whether he was more embarrassed to see me, or if I was more surprised to see Tom as a cop. After a quick and incomplete mini-reunion to break the tension, Tom asked if I knew why he had been pulled me over. Of course, I did. He said he was sorry, but he was writing me a ticket for speeding. I admit he gave me a bit of a break on the actual speed he recorded on the ticket, but Tom did his job. Before he left me to get back to the police car, he asked if I wanted to get a cup of coffee at the end of his shift. I agreed to meet him later that day.

When we met, Tom filled me in on how and why he became a cop. He'd gotten into a lot of minor trouble after we parted in high school—nothing too serious.

One of the good things about living in a small town is that not much changes. So every time Tom was taken into custody, it was by the same local police officer. Another thing about living in a small town is the local jail is not a very active place. An occasional drunk or a jaywalker or stupid kid with bad judgment were the jail's only patrons. After Tom kept showing up there, the local police officer took the occasions to talk with Tom about his past and his future.

Because of those talks, that local cop persuaded Tom to get his GED and to apply, with his recommendation, to become a policeman. Tom got a kick out of the irony of all of that. And so Tom, following the encouragement of our local policeman, completed a GED, applied, and was accepted to train to become a local cop. He excelled in his police training.

At the same time, Tom was encouraged to go back to church. The same priest who used to bail him out of jail when we were in high school was still at the same church. The priest invited Tom back to explore faith and its place in Tom's life. While attending church, Tom met a girl who he later married. They already had one young child, a boy.

Tom concluded our coffee session with this summary of what he believes happened to him. If it hadn't been for the interest and guidance he received from the local policeman, his life would have followed the path he had been on toward real criminal activity, or perhaps worse. A representative of the law saved him from potential harm. Tom also understood that his priest played a large part in changing his life. He had been saved by faith. The local priest, a representative of what faith could mean in one's life, became a part of Tom's new journey in life.

Tom also learned to trust and embrace the love he felt for his wife and young son as a crucial component in his efforts to become a better person.

Every time he looked at his boy, he remembered his own childhood and daily prayed that, unlike how his parents treated him, he would always care for and encourage his young son. His wife was devoted to Tom and their son, helping Tom to experience the transforming power of love.

Tom remembered the pain and suffering he had as a kid and a young adult. Those memories were always present with him. But Tom knew that he had been saved by the law, his faith, and the power of transforming love. The suffering he had experienced never left, but he had found redemption, salvation, and a way to a new start in life.

Having What It Takes

Similarly, in 1 Peter 4, we see the power of salvation, love, and right behavior as reasons to be obedient to God and Jesus. Let's look at this chapter in three sections:

1. 1 Peter 4:1–6
2. 1 Peter 4:7–11
3. 1 Peter 4:12–19

First, Peter's message to prospective converts was to decide if they were strong enough in their spirit to endure the sacrifice and suffering following Jesus would require. Those of you who have been faithfully reading along in scripture probably wonder why Peter kept stressing suffering for the faith. Didn't his followers, followers of Jesus, get it by now? Peter answered in 1 Peter 4:3–4:

> You have already spent enough time in doing what the Gentiles like to do, living in licentiousness, passions, drunkenness, revels, carousing, and lawless idolatry. They are surprised that you no longer join them in the same excesses of dissipation, and so they blaspheme.

There were two types of suffering that Jews, Gentiles, and followers of Jesus were experiencing. The first was the overall suffering of any person singled out and persecuted for a lifestyle contrary to religious and civil leaders' laws. At that time, bodily persecution or martyrdom was almost certain for any person or group that acted in opposition to religious or civil authority. This form of suffering attacked one's mind and body.

The second form of suffering was living in a society surrounded by people who appeared to be enjoying all that life had to offer, unconstrained by behaviors prohibited by one's adherence to Jesus' teachings. Followers of Christ were tempted continually by others who were only too happy to lead these new Christians astray, back to former lives of excess and selfishness. This form of suffering attacked one's spirit.

Folks who had previously heard Peter's reassurance concerning suffering for the sake of doing God's will found some purpose, some reason for their suffering. They knew by following Jesus' example, they would suffer and endure for their faith and beliefs because Jesus had suffered and endured for his. They would find release from their suffering through their faith and service to others just as Jesus found freedom from his suffering on the cross. According to God's will, suffering as a follower of Christ freed followers to begin a new way of life.

As he taught, Peter was even more direct in his message, "for whoever has suffered in the flesh has finished with sin." (1 Peter 4:1) If one is accused of doing wrong for having done what is right in God's eyes, God will bless them, and they are "finished with sin." But if one continues in current behaviors, as did the Gentiles, not caring about obeying God's will, sin's corrupting power will remain. Peter spoke of a time when God would judge all people. Those who suffered because of their intentional sin and those who suffered for doing what was right would both receive God's promised judgment. For the sake of Jesus, suffering in the name of Jesus found its reward in salvation and eternal life. God would be with all those who sacrificed and suffered for following God's will. Unless encouraged to confess their sins and repent freely, those who engaged in un-Christlike behaviors (as was the conduct of many Gentiles), would find ultimate judgment waiting for them on the promised day of judgment.

In 1 Peter 4:7–11, folks heard a message of what to think and how to behave while waiting for the return of Christ to earth. This message was for the benefit of folks who had recently accepted life as a follower of Christ. They still had much to learn, and they still had to test their faith in the real world and in their daily lives. When Jesus returned, many believed and trusted their sacrifices and suffering would end.

Peter and others preached that Jesus would return soon and gather up faithful followers. Most folks assumed that Jesus would return in their lifetime, at which time they would have their reward for being faithful followers of Christ.

The Second Coming had been postponed; the Messiah had not returned. False teachers and false prophets seized on the seeming inconsistency of the timing and lack of certainty concerning Jesus' return. Some of those same false teachers preached that Jesus was gone for good, and they, therefore, possessed the true message that folks should follow. To suffer while waiting for Jesus' return was not the message the false teachers and false prophets offered. Instead, they offered a way of living far less demanding than what Peter taught. And most importantly, following the false prophets meant there would probably be little persecution and harassment by civil or religious authorities.

What kept everyone from deserting the quest to follow Jesus (who was conspicuously absent) and joining the followers of very present and accessible false teachers? There are all sorts of reasons a person decides to follow the dictates or teachings of a particular teacher or prophet. In your own life, I am sure you have had to make decisions between those in whom you could place your confidence and trust, and those in whom you had less confidence.

People listened to Peter because he was an original disciple of Jesus and had studied directly under Jesus. You also remember Jesus selected Peter as the one who would build Christ's church. That church would become the foundation of Christian theology and worship. Very few questioned Peter's authority to preach in the name of Jesus. There was little doubt Peter could be trusted and believed.

Peter was filled with the Holy Spirit. He had suffered for his faith. Peter spoke from his direct knowledge of what was demanded of Jesus' followers. Very few came close to his qualifications as one whose words could be trusted. By the Holy Spirit's power, Peter and his "students" received the authority to preach the challenges and rewards one faced as a follower of Christ.

1 Peter 4:7 opens this section: "The end of all things is near, therefore be serious and discipline yourselves for the sake of your prayers." One did not come to times of prayer to have casual conversation with God. Those early Christians did not presume they had the right or the standing to engage God in worship or prayer without seriousness of purpose—the purpose being to discover and experience how ordinary believers would accomplish God's will. One's prayers asked for that right and standing to act and witness to others so that God would be known and worshiped.

Those requirements to act in the name of Jesus for the sake of God are found in 1 Peter 4:8–11. As you reread those three verses, consider how you provide evidence by your actions and your words concerning the change in your life since you became a follower of Jesus. People watch you just as surely as they watched each other in the days of the early church.

As people watch you go about your daily tasks, what kind of person will they see? Will they believe your actions and attitudes to be those of a follower of Jesus? What will others see in you as you lead them to consider Christ in their lives? Are you a believable witness to the goodness and transforming power found in following Jesus?

Although many found the behaviors and attitudes in 1 Peter 4:8–11 challenging to follow, Peter did not ask for the impossible. It was those new behaviors: loving one another, offering hospitality, and serving others, that defined and identified a follower of Christ. One ought to be ready to live in such a way that the reality of suffering and persecution of professing Christians would not be sufficient reason to dissuade followers from faithful obedience to Christ and his commands. Therefore, reasons to suffer had to be considered and accepted if believers were to endure. Peter suggested believers find joy in suffering by imitating the very behaviors and beliefs Jesus practiced. Jesus found joy and purpose in his suffering as he went about teaching, healing, and transforming lives. You and I might also find similar joy and purpose in our suffering, as we share the Good News we have heard. In fact, discovering and accepting reasons for joy in suffering might be the very place to begin our journeys of faith.

1 Peter 4:11 is of particular importance to this section: "Whoever speaks must do so as one speaking the very words of God ...." This attitude and guidance affected how believers spoke and listened to each other. Peter showed his humility as he gave God the glory for what he said and did.

But at the same time, the false teachers had another agenda—to promote their teaching and to promote people joining their groups. Just an aside, the false teachers existed because of their cleverness and how they used their ability to influence crowds for the benefit of the false teachers. They held on to glory for themselves rather than returning it to God and Jesus. It was they, not God, who put whatever power and authority they claimed in their teachings, all the while demanding acceptance and trust from those who followed them.

The third section of this chapter highlights 1 Peter 4:12–19. The whole of this section can be summed up in verse 19: "Therefore, let those suffering in accordance with God's will entrust themselves to a faithful Creator while continuing to do good."

We have already discovered a reason for suffering while doing the will of God, even as Jesus suffered to fulfill God's will. But suffering while doing God's work, if done with an insincere or casual attitude, denied followers the real reward of suffering, the joy of casting off selfish desires and actions for a greater purpose.

Followers of Jesus are constantly challenged to do what is right and honorable in their relationships and dealings with others. According to scripture, new converts are commanded to act and discipline themselves according to a lifestyle and behaviors that bring honor to God and give evidence of new life in Christ for others to see and consider for themselves. Because of those demands, it is also hopeful to hear and believe the words of 1 Peter 4:14: "If you are reviled for the name of Christ, you are blessed, because the Spirit of glory which is the Spirit of God, is resting on you." This verse only makes sense if we are willing to accept that the Holy Spirit guides us and encourages us toward righteous and holy living as we freely give our lives to Christ through baptism, worship, and service to others. We are new people in Christ.

Rewards of Faithful Obedience Turned to Joy

When it comes to the power of encouragement, I keep thinking back to my friend Tom, who found his life had been changed forever when he was encouraged, acknowledged, nurtured, and finally held accountable for his actions. Tom followed a new path and survived many challenges. He would go on to share his story with others he met, pointing out how he found his strength in his faith in God and Jesus. Tom was a believable voice to many who heard him speak or who came under his care. He volunteered lots of time to shelters for runaway kids, programs for abused teens, and mentoring juvenile offenders.

It might be helpful to consider what life held out for folks in the early church who found Jesus' example so compelling. Those folks labored under the often brutal yoke of religious and civil domination. Life for most folks in first-century times offered little variety. From Jesus' birth, the world in Bethlehem, Jerusalem, Nazareth, Galilee, and surrounding towns had been filled with rumors and gossip concerning the sometimes radical but always life-changing teachings of Jesus. To the folks living then, Jesus was said to be either the long-awaited Messiah who came to set people free or a dangerous revolutionary who antagonized religious and civil leaders. There was no middle ground, no safe passage in the journey with Jesus. So choosing to follow Jesus or not was not a casual decision.

Peter spoke in 1 Peter 4:17: "For the time has come for judgment to begin with the household of God; if it begins with us, what will be the end for those who do not obey the gospel of God?" Peter reminded followers of Jesus of the coming judgment. Those who had chosen Christ and lived obediently, according to his commandments, would find salvation, and be blessed with eternal life in heaven. Those who had heard the Gospel message but did not heed the words of Peter and other teachers and prophets of the Word would be harshly judged and spend an eternity in the fires of hell.

My friend Tom had his life forever changed, but it did not end there. Throughout the rest of his life, he dedicated himself to doing good, encouraging the young, and seeking to protect the weak. His life was not free from all difficulty or suffering, yet it was a life lived in joyful obedience to the lessons he had learned from those who cared enough to offer him a new way.

This life of joyful obedience is what Christ offered the people of the early church. Living with this attitude is the life and the choice Christ still holds out for all people. And in turn, it becomes the responsibility of followers of Christ, you and me, to offer the message of Good News, of new life following Jesus, to all we meet. Followers of Christ find joy inviting and encouraging others to begin their own journey of faith and discovery. Do you believe this?

Further Consideration and Action

As you think back on this chapter, consider the shift in tone from anxiety and doubt to joy and salvation found in the teachings of Christ and the message of Peter.

There are many places in the Bible where it is clear we are being commanded rather than guided, as in the Ten Commandments (Exodus 20:2-17 and Deuteronomy 5:6-21) or the Great Commission (Matthew 28:16-20). Even the Beatitudes (found in Matthew 5:3–12), which seem at first glance to suggest a moral and ethical life, really direct the behaviors Christians should be known for and include in their lives.

- All that said, in what ways do you believe Christ is commanding or directing you to follow the life and ministry of Jesus?
- How does following Jesus affect how you see yourself and how you interact with others, especially others that seek to harm you or cause you to suffer?
- As Christians, what are the sacrifices required of you as you interact with others?
- What part does free will have in your ability to choose your own behaviors and attitudes toward others and toward following Jesus?

We discussed Peter's power and presence and his authority to speak in God's name based on his position as one of the original disciples. Yet Peter and the other disciples could not successfully preach or teach or heal in Jesus' name until after Pentecost when the Holy Spirit came upon all assembled. Jesus provided his ministry as a living example of what it meant to serve God's will through obedient service. For followers of Christ, the Holy Spirit must have been a necessary component in helping others.

- How would you define or describe the Holy Spirit's purpose in empowering teachers and preachers and followers of Jesus?
- What does it mean to have the Holy Spirit rest upon you?
- If you have experienced the Holy Spirit at work in your life, describe what led you to believe the Spirit was at work in you?

In 1 Peter 4:8–11, Peter outlined behaviors and attitudes followers of Jesus should adopt and encourage in others as they patiently wait for the "end of all things." Followers are instructed to be serious and disciplined, maintain a love for one another, and offer hospitality to all. Further, they are to be good stewards of the gifts and talents they have received from God. Jesus' followers are to take care as they use their words since they "speak the very words of God" when having conversations with others. Finally, Peter taught that whoever serves another must do so with all their body, mind, and spirit so that all they do will bring glory and honor to God.

- How might these expectations affect your life?
- What additional encouragement would you need to live by the guidance provided in 1 Peter 4:8-11?
- How might it be easier for you if you were held accountable for your behaviors by a small group of like-minded believers?

In 1 Peter 4:18, Peter reminds his listeners of the dire consequences of neglecting their call to bring others to Christ. Peter said, "If it is hard for the righteous to be saved, what will become of the ungodly and sinners?" I have often asked folks this question when talking about salvation: "You are saved from what, to what?" Just what is salvation?

Being saved isn't a get-out-of-jail-free card. Experiencing salvation is to know because of the love of God, the sacrifice of his Son, and the sustaining power of the Holy Spirit, you are equipped and ready for service in God's name. You have been saved from your former life to a new life guided by the Holy Spirit. In this change, you willingly surrender to a life saved from sin and temptation, a life of obedient service that brings honor and glory to God. In a sense, through the sacrifice of Jesus on the cross, you too have been freed from fear and the power of sin and death. This new freedom allows you to confidently go about living and preaching the Good News in harmony with the behaviors and expectations you have read in Peter's first letter.

- Take a moment to consider this question—do you believe this? Do you believe you have been saved from the behaviors and beliefs of your past and present life freeing you to accept the call to new behaviors and new ministry for your future? To what end will you accept the gift of salvation?
- What will it take for you to claim your salvation and accept your call to be known as a follower of Jesus?
- What do you need in your life to go out and make new disciples for Christ?

We are commanded to bring glory to God through our service and our witness to God's love for all people.

- Where in your home, your church, and your community is this service or witness needed?
- What's your plan to fulfill those needs?

Chapter Six

Good Behaviors to Adopt

I ENCOURAGE YOU TO grab your journal again. Keep track of questions and other points you might wish to review or study more in-depth. Before reading this chapter, read 1 Peter 5:1–14.

> Let us pray:
> Gracious Lord, you have called us to care for one another according to the gifts and talents you have given each of us. By your Holy Spirit, help us live lives that bring glory to you so that by our actions, people will know of our trust and faith in you. Cause us to act as one family, one community, united by the example of your Son, Jesus, in whose name we pray. Amen.

In my life before being ordained as a pastor, I was a teacher, coach, counselor, and administrator at various independent schools, I have been blessed by teaching alongside many men and women who are exceptional people. What I mean by "exceptional people" are folks who always have the best interest of their students in mind. They see their job as nurturing, affirming, and encouraging their students.

Students are particularly good at seeing past the outward appearances and false bravado of their teachers. They can quickly identify those teachers who see what they do as "just a job." Great teachers describe teaching as a vital calling, a humbling challenge, an almost sacred reverence of offering new insight and understanding to the students entrusted to their care.

Some characteristics of exceptional teachers are authenticity, a love for their chosen field of study, humility, compassion, patience, and a sense of urgency concerning the sharing of knowledge inside and outside the classroom setting. Again, students quickly come to sense those teachers who care and who can be trusted and believed.

Great teachers are great leaders. Part encourager, part wise sage, part dreamer, part role model, master teachers mix their subject matter with practical application. Great teachers bring their subject matter to life, teaching lessons that lead to noble pursuits. Great teachers inspire, share strategy, and craft a vision resulting in new insight, discovery, and direction.

Likewise, as a full-time pastor for the last twenty years, I have had the opportunity to mentor several young pastors. Those young folks were in the process of answering a call to ministry. In my denomination, men and women who attend seminary and earn a master's degree in theology and ministry are appointed to a church as a pastor—a modern-day shepherd of a flock.

Just as with an exceptional teacher, an outstanding pastor is a humble leader. He or she is dedicated, authentic, vulnerable, and a steadfast and faithful example of what it means to be a Christian. Outstanding pastors are identified as trustworthy leaders because of the compatibility of what they teach and preach and how they behave in their everyday lives.

In their way, teachers and pastors humbly go about the rigorous pursuit of imparting knowledge. They suggest the practical application of how their knowledge and understanding may benefit others. Both professions are about touching lives, opening new possibilities, and perhaps even transforming people's lives. Teachers and pastors lead by the depth of their convictions, their fundamental values, and their belief in what they teach. Exceptional teachers and preachers are believable. They can be counted on to communicate the truth found in scripture or the truth found in their particular academic area of expertise.

We've arrived at the last chapter of Peter's first letter. In addressing the elders of the community, folks who have fully committed to a life of serving in Jesus' name, Peter reminds them of the responsibility and obligation they have taken upon themselves. These elders freely chose to enter positions of leadership. They answered the call to serve as living examples or witnesses of the change they have experienced as a result of their faith and trust in God and Jesus Christ. Their unwavering faith in God and Jesus is a large part of what they share with those in their care. Educating youth and leading them to find faith in Christ is their noble purpose, the life-affirming work of the elders in the community. They are the teachers entrusted with the ethical and moral character of the next generation.

Humility in the Presence of God

Peter cautioned both elders and new converts to be humble in their relationships. What's behind Peter's message to those under his care to practice humility in their relationships with others? Peter came to realize that for a follower of Jesus, all one has, all that one is, all that one accomplishes is the result of accepting God's gifts and blessings. These gifts and blessings are then to be used to benefit others, giving all the glory to God and Jesus.

The accomplishments of God's people are not the result of their power or status or training. It is God at work through faithful and obedient individuals. 1 Peter 5:6 points out: "Humble yourselves therefore under the mighty hand of God, so that he may exalt you in due time." This sense of humility, acknowledging God's power in one's life, while depending on God-given wisdom, is a necessary characteristic of a religious teacher. This kind of teacher passes on the truth of the Word of God, as well as the attitudes and behaviors seen in the life and ministry of Jesus Christ. Believers are reminded in 1 Peter 5:7, "Cast all your anxiety on him, because he cares for you." The God who created you has equipped you with all the necessary talent you need to humbly serve and assist others, all the while giving glory to God.

Peter then turned his attention back to the suffering elders and their followers would undoubtedly face. In 1 Peter 5:8, we read, "Discipline yourselves, keep alert. Like a roaring lion, your adversary the devil prowls around, looking for someone to devour." Exactly what is the threat to others from people who follow Jesus Christ? Why are they met with so much anger, misunderstanding, and persecution?

It's not always easy to talk about or understand evil and the devil. Whatever your understanding of the concept of the devil, you have probably met people in your life who are unkind, jealous, abusive, judgmental, or just plain hurtful toward you and others. Some people cannot stand to be seen as not as good as you are, not as smart, not as popular, or not as calm as you. And so they respond to you in hurtful and demeaning ways. But by attempting to diminish you, these hurtful folks only succeed in diminishing themselves. Your faith gives you strength they can never possess.

Individuals who demean, injure, and malign others are the bullies in our lives. They lash out in an attempt to harm us. And no matter how strong or self-aware we are, too many times we suffer at their hands. Peter reminded us to pay attention to the devil in 1 Peter 5:9, "Resist him, steadfast in your faith, for you know that your brothers and sisters in all the world are undergoing the same kinds of suffering." Once again, you and I are not alone in our faith in Jesus. It is essential to surround ourselves with a like-minded community of believers who pray for others who have not found the same hope and peace of mind we have as followers of Christ.

By now, you know Peter has Good News for those who suffer for the sake of the Gospel. By the grace of God, we are promised there is an end to our suffering. You and I can begin to understand this promise in the example of Jesus' victory over his own suffering. Jesus re-discovered his faith and his purpose while on the cross. Jesus, as he surrendered his Spirit to God, cried out, "It is finished." His suffering found its end when he completed what God had called him to do.

Our suffering finds its conclusion when we discover, accept, surrender, and finish what God has called us to accomplish in our lives. We can discover our purpose through study, prayer, questioning, doubting, and asking for help from the company of folks we trust and believe to be faithful followers of Jesus.

This section of the chapter comes to its end in the words of 1 Peter 5:10, "And after you have suffered for a little while, the God of all grace, who has called you to his eternal glory in Christ, will himself restore, support, strengthen, and establish you." Let those words sink in. God has not and will not abandon you or me or leave us alone in the challenges we face.

Just as Jesus suffered and found release from that suffering, so too do believers like you and me find relief as we live faithful, obedient lives. Believers realize that suffering is temporary. Our suffering can be endured because of God's promise of an end to that suffering for those who are steadfast in their faith and trust in the words and example of Jesus Christ. Members of the "household of God," our brothers and sisters in Christ, persevere and endure suffering in service to God and Jesus.

The final verse in this section is 1 Peter 5:11, "To him be the power forever and ever. Amen." God's power begins in God's love for us and in God's protection of us even while we suffer. God never leaves us alone as we surrender our lives to be born anew in Christ. Just as Christ endured his suffering through his steadfast faith in God, we, too, by our faith in Jesus and God's love, can find peace and joy even as we suffer for our faith.

It's a sign of a mature Christian who realizes that when the clouds of suffering or other adversity are lifted, our faith is renewed. Just as our gifts and talents are from God, so most surely, it is by God's power and mercy, God's love and forgiveness, that we as individuals or members of a community of believers can endure suffering as we continue our lifelong journey of faith.

This understanding and witness of faith results in words, thoughts, and deeds, possibly leading others to ask us questions about our faith in Christ. Our faith, our witness, is testimony to the responsibilities and obligations we take on as those who will follow in the ministry we learned at the hands of faithful teachers. Just as early Christians were taught and led by Peter, we are the recipients of the wisdom and knowledge of those who lead us to Christ.

Peter spent his ministry in an attempt to communicate his experience, wrestling with his faith, and what he was inspired and moved to share in the name of Christ with new converts and followers of Jesus. Not all who heard Peter teach believed what he had to say. There were others in the crowds who heard Peter's message but were unconvinced.

Peter wasn't able to deliver this letter in person, so he entrusted it to his student and friend Silvanus (or Silas). Peter hoped his communication would encourage those who heard it. Peter made his final plea to the crowds restating his unique qualifications to serve as a reliable witness of what he experienced as one of the original disciples of Christ. Peter's life had been forever changed, and in that change, he had found peace and calm, even a sense of joy, amidst his suffering and ultimate martyrdom. His joy was in following Christ's path, even as he put aside his desires and his temptations.

The Power of Words

These days, not many folks write letters. We either text or email. Our communications with one another are short and specific. Remember that Peter wrote to churches he had once visited or had a hand in establishing. You also remember that Peter and the other disciples didn't stay in any place for too long before religious and civil authorities became threatened by the unsettling teachings the disciples shared. In particular, Peter felt called to share his testimony with as many people as possible so that the Good News of Jesus Christ might unite folks by their shared faith and belief in Jesus. Don't forget the followers of Jesus were almost always seen as threats to those most in danger of losing their positions, power, and authority.

For those religious and civil authorities who felt threatened, Jesus' death was thought to have ended or at least diminished the disturbances and restlessness caused by Jesus and his followers. But no amount of persecution of early Christians would end trouble for those religious and civil authorities. When Peter and other preachers came to town sharing the Good News of a life following Jesus, there was no choice but to silence them. There was always the risk of being thrown into jail, persecuted, or martyred for sharing testimony based on Jesus' teachings and ministry. There was still a need for encouragement from faithful, Spirit-filled teachers and prophets, like Peter.

To stay in contact with communities where he had preached, Peter (and his students) wrote their letters of encouragement and assurance to those who had decided for Christ. Messages were often delivered by a follower or student of a particular disciple or traveling preacher. This behavior was risky for the messenger as well as the one who wrote the letters. Many letters ended with a blessing or prayer, just as does this letter, "Peace to all of you who are in Christ." This phrase is the essence of the faith journey—to find Christ's peace, a peace that passes all understanding and brings hope to faithful followers of the Good News.

Further Consideration and Action

The practical demands of being a follower of Jesus were great. One's behaviors, words, and actions toward others were under constant scrutiny by prospective converts as well as the watchful eyes and ears of the ever-present civil and religious authorities. Additionally, false prophets or teachers of false doctrine were continually lurking about, waiting to step in at any sign of spiritual weakness among believers to subvert the true meaning of following Jesus as taught by Peter and his disciples.

Against all of this was the steadfast, faith-filled witness of Peter. His mission and purpose were clear. Peter's vulnerability and his willingness to sacrifice even his life for the Good News of Jesus Christ provided a real-time example of the joys and the challenges of being a follower of Jesus.

As you consider the questions that follow, imagine being encouraged by Peter all the while being discouraged and manipulated or abused by those in opposition to Peter's teachings. Who would you have followed? What encouragement would you need on your journey of faith? What encouragement might you provide others?

Peter took care to remind folks that he was one of the original disciples, and as such, his words and his witness were accurate and could be believed. He had suffered for being a follower of Christ. Yet even under the threats of persecution and imprisonment, Peter went on preaching and teaching. And people responded to Peter's words and his qualifications as a disciple of Christ.

- Today, what qualifies a person to speak on God's behalf?
- In these days of fake news and church-related scandals, what would it take for you to believe and trust the testimony of someone who claims to speak the truth—God's truth?

Peter encouraged followers of Christ to examine themselves and discover the gifts God had given them. He invited believers to thank God for those gifts and to employ those skills with a humble spirit and in humble service.

- What are your gifts, your skills, your talents?
- How will you discover your God-given talents and how those talents might be of use to you and others? As a Christian what is your mission, your purpose?
- How do you serve God's people who may be suffering, especially spiritual suffering?
- How might you share your belief and trust in Jesus with others?

Peter warns folks about the power of evil and the devil. The devil tempts believers away from their faith.

- What would draw you away from your faith in Jesus?
- How do you experience the devil, and how do you resist the devil's temptations?
- Were false prophets at work on behalf of the devil?
- Why is evil so powerful?
- Are there present-day agents of evil at work? How can believers recognize those people and their threats?

In 1 Peter 5:10, we read, "And after you have suffered for a little while, the God of all grace, who has called you to his eternal glory in Christ, will himself restore, support, strengthen, and establish you." This verse reassures some readers. They understand it to mean that God is present right now in their lives. Some people understand this verse to suggest that God's actions will occur in the future.

- How do you interpret this verse?
- When have you felt comforted, supported, or protected from the suffering believers undergo for the sake of the Gospel message?

Write a letter to a close friend. Send them words of encouragement and an assurance that they are not alone in life. Share some brief testimony with your friend, summarizing why you believe in the Good News of Jesus Christ. Help them consider that though we all suffer at some point in our lives, there may be reasons for suffering, which, when understood, can free us to better endure our suffering and sacrifice.

Chapter Seven

Discovering the Power of
Your Words and Actions

THIS CHAPTER BEGINS Peter's second letter. Record your thoughts and reflections in your journal. And be sure to read 2 Peter 1:1–21 before beginning this chapter.

> Let us pray:
> May the words of my mouth and the meditations of my heart find acceptance with you, O Lord, my strength and redeemer. Amen.

I saw a Facebook post the other day, and I'm paraphrasing the message, but it said, "If you are attending a church that is teaching you to hate or judge others, find yourselves a new church."

I wondered why any pastor or minister of a Christian church would teach their members to hate or believe that some people aren't welcome in church. I also wondered why any Christian would continue to go to a church that preached that judging and excluding some folks from membership was acceptable. Why was this social media meme even necessary to post?

I look back at the churches I attended growing up. Sadly I have to say that while the message was not overt, there was a common perception in town that my "home" church wasn't necessarily welcoming to all people in that community. It dawned on me there were many Christian churches in my town from which to choose. They all defined themselves as worshiping and believing in Jesus Christ. Within walking distance of the church I attended (a reasonably conservative Presbyterian Church), there was also a United Methodist Church, an Episcopal Church, a Baptist Church, an A.M.E. Church, three Catholic Churches, and various Bible-based Churches. *Weren't all Christian churches Bible-based?* Adding to the mix in my town, there was also a Jewish Temple and a Society of Friends Meeting House. *Didn't they, too, study scripture?*

As a young kid, I never really grasped why there were so many different "flavors" of worshiping Jesus and so many ways to understand scripture. I just knew that my family and the folks I knew all went to the same church. All the other churches seemed shrouded in mystery and were a bit suspect in theology and their practices. At least that's what I was told in Sunday School.

Every summer, my church and the adjacent Methodist Church held joint Sunday morning worship services. One month at one church, the next at the other, and then back to the familiar. We sang different hymns, prayed different prayers, and Methodist sermons seemed shorter than my minister's sermons. In both churches, Jesus was mentioned a great deal, as was the Bible. Talk of the eternal fires of hell was more prevalent in the sermons at the church I attended. Something called grace seemed to be the Methodist mantra. Methodists seemed to believe God loved them. My church presented God as one who was continually judging us and our behaviors.

During my faith journey, I have attended tent revivals, Pentecostal services, snake-handling church services, and worship services lasting three or four hours with loud music and dancing. Jesus was always in there someplace. At least that's what members of those worship communities told me.

Now that I am an adult, it has become clear that among the pastors I know and have served with, we preach and teach quite different variations of similar themes, all in the same denomination. The other thing about my denomination is that we pastors move a great deal—it's called itinerancy. Going from one church to another in the same denomination should be easy. But no, one church wants me to preach about Jesus and the old stories. Another wants me to preach about missions, another social activism. Nowadays, in some churches, I can preach openly about LGBTQ+ issues. In others, I would be asked to leave if I offered any support for "sinful lifestyles." Regardless of where I am, I preach the same message—the Good News of Jesus Christ. It's amazing (and somewhat disappointing) how people interpret my sermon to affirm or deny what they believe they have heard me preach.

Entire churches have followed their pastor out the door and into a new building because they were put off by the subtle messages of denominational directives to advocate for issues that a particular congregation did not believe. The church's understanding of scripture and the sermons they heard did not coincide with the guidance from denominational authorities. We Christians seem fiercely independent when it comes to our religious opinions and preferences. Isn't one of our greatest strengths supposed to be unity in Jesus Christ? There is a quote (whose authorship is in dispute) that is supposed to give us guidance concerning our beliefs: "in essentials, unity; in doubtful matters, liberty; and in all things, charity." It is a struggle many of us have experienced to know what to believe, who to believe, and how to believe. This has caused much confusion for people who are trying to find something in which to believe.

So where is the truth of Jesus Christ preached? As a kid, I was taught this song: "Jesus loves me this I know, for the Bible tells me so. Little ones to him belong. We are weak, but he is strong. Yes, Jesus loves me, the Bible tells me so." And I thought everyone believed that. That's what I was told. I was taught to trust the Word of God—the Holy Bible.

Yet I saw and heard some terrible things coming from the mouths and behaviors of fellow church members. I was shocked at the reactions of some who sat near my family each Sunday morning. I wondered if Jesus loved them. I wondered how Jesus could love them. They seemed full of judgment and hatred.

Then came the late sixties. There was terrible violence occurring between white Christians and Black Christians. Jesus' little children were dying. What Gospel message was being preached that made all of that okay?

There are false teachers and false prophets of the Gospel. False prophets and teachers also showed up early on in the Old Testament. Such false teachers' and preachers' agendas did not necessarily coincide with the plan Jesus left for his followers.

Followers of Jesus Christ, who confidently declared themselves Christians, confused me as a kid and even today as an adult. The actions and words of these confident Christians didn't always match Jesus' teaching. Where are prophets and preachers like Peter or Paul when you need them? Those two particular teachers and prophets seemed to have a good handle on what it meant to be a faithful follower of Christ. Perhaps it was because they had direct experience and knowledge of Jesus and his message. It's good to be reminded from time to time what it means to call oneself a Christian. Studying the New Testament and what it means to be a Christian is an essential part of one's journey of faith and understanding.

Grace and Peace

Peter's second letter to the people under his care began with these essential words found in 2 Peter 1:2, "May grace and peace be yours in abundance in the knowledge of God and Jesus our Lord." Hundreds of sermons and prayers have been written and preached with that verse as the central theme. Imagine if this was the way we Christians greeted each other on Sunday mornings.

In many churches, members are asked to "pass the peace" to other church-goers as a sign of what unites us. Passing the peace is a simple handshake and acknowledgment of the presence of another follower of Christ. Just as Jesus offered all he met grace and peace, so should we be willing to make this sign of welcome and hospitality to our fellow Christian brothers and sisters.

Through his example, Jesus made it clear that we should not reserve grace and peace just for fellow Christians but that we should offer those gifts to *all* people. The ancient church grew when Gentiles and Jews were invited into fellowship and hospitality in Jesus' name. All were invited and welcomed to hear what life in Christ offered. Offering grace and peace to one another meant providing a safe place to worship and to have conversation. A place of grace and peace, the church, was where what Jesus taught was passed on to others.

The next section of the reading is from 2 Peter 1:3. Here Peter described a foundation of belief and motivation directing the actions and behaviors of followers of Christ. Just as Peter spent so much time in the last letter discussing the inevitability of suffering for one's faith in Jesus, he now takes time to outline behaviors and beliefs that are essential to those who wish to follow Jesus and develop their faith and trust in his ministry.

Peter's preaching demonstrated practical applications of Jesus' theology so that new followers of Christ would have a model to help make sense of their world. Peter taught that Jesus' followers already had received all they would need to adopt Christlike standards. Living as a Christian depended on accepting Jesus' promises of righteous living, repentance, salvation, and the certainty of eternal life for his faithful and obedient followers.

Peter taught that those under his care would grow in faith and gain confidence as Christians as they discovered and experienced what a life following Jesus would provide. By practicing goodness, gaining knowledge of Jesus, exercising self-control, enduring all trials, living in godliness, showing mutual affection for all believers, and loving all, followers of Christ would learn to develop faith and trust in a new way of living.

The faith of those who followed Christ was strengthened in living by Christian expectations, providing a tangible, day-to-day witness so others could understand what a life in Christ looked like. Words and actions both mattered. Followers grew to find purpose in their faith. This gave them the confidence to live out their faith despite the challenges, sacrifices, and hardships following Christ would require.

Most of those virtues, more fully described in Galatians 5:22 as the fruits of the Spirit, are what Peter and others taught as being consistent with Jesus' teaching and example. Those virtues were: love, joy, peace, patience, kindness, goodness, faithfulness, gentleness, and self-control. Godliness and holy living were defined as learning to live by standards set by God and Jesus. These are behaviors that have the power to transform lives. Godliness is a life of reverence and obedience to the way of life shown to us in the example of Jesus. Mutual affection and love was Peter's teaching to those early converts, imploring them to strive to care not only for fellow believers but also those who had been forgotten, marginalized, or pushed aside. During his short time in ministry,

Jesus reached out with love to women and children, to sinners, and to outcasts. Peter commended those behaviors to newly converted followers of Christ.

It's Peter's teaching that all who accept Jesus as Lord and Savior are called to a life of service in Jesus' name. Those who accept Jesus as Lord are set apart or empowered to invite others to Christ, not by manipulation or peer pressure, but as a response to the personal example of new life following in Christ's footsteps. In 1 Peter 2:9, we heard the directive:

> But you are a chosen race, a royal priesthood, a holy nation, God's own people, in order that you might proclaim the mighty acts of him who called you out of darkness into his marvelous light.

Peter had something similar in mind. In 2 Peter 1:11, he reminded folks of the transforming power of this new life, "For in this way, entry into the eternal kingdom of our Lord and Savior Jesus Christ will be richly provided for you." Peter is reminding followers that just as they will suffer for their faith as did Christ, believers will also find an eternal reward in heaven, just as Christ did.

Peter concluded this instruction in 2 Peter 1:12,15, "Therefore I intend to keep on reminding you of these things, though you know them already and are established in the truth that has come to you." He continued, "And I will make every effort so that after my departure you may be able at any time to recall these things."

Peter began to hint at a time when he would depart from those he had been teaching. Peter's departure might point to a specific time when he will leave his followers to continue in his ministry, or it might suggest his impending persecution, imprisonment, and death. Peter is clear, however, that his time is coming to an end.

Peter instructed his students to carry his message forward after he was gone. Without a direct connection to Peter's witness of what he had learned at Jesus' feet, the Gospel message might surely have lost its impact and believability. The false prophets waited to take advantage of any weakness in the Gospel being preached by Peter's students. And so Peter authorized his students, led by the Holy Spirit, to teach and preach the Good News. In that way, Peter's students were able to ensure that his message would pass on to future generations of curious seekers of the Gospel.

Peter's actions authorized future teachers to preach with the same Spirit-filled authority Peter had possessed. Some churches call this transfer of the power and authority of the Spirit "apostolic succession." This succession or transfer of authority is simply a recognition that the truth of Jesus' words can only be taught by those who can trace their authority to speak in Jesus' name back to Jesus or one of the original twelve disciples.

In today's church, this transfer of a Spirit-filled ability to preach and teach with authority occurs when folks are ordained or set apart for this task. At ordination, the Spirit is passed down from generation to generation as teachers lay hands on their students. From that time on, these new teachers and preachers are able to share the Gospel message in Jesus' name.

Peter reiterated his credentials to drive home his authority to speak on behalf of what he had witnessed during the three years he traveled with Jesus. Remember, Jesus appointed Peter to be the Rock, the foundation for Jesus' church. But Peter's words to the crowds were, "For we did not follow cleverly devised myths when we made known to you the power and coming of our Lord Jesus Christ, but we had been eyewitnesses of his majesty." (2 Peter 1:16) Peter was already aware of false teachers' influence and false prophets spreading their versions of Jesus' ministry. He wanted to be clear that those who heard his words would not doubt those words' authority and integrity.

In the end, Peter offered his followers final words about his testimony concerning Jesus' ministry. He said in 2 Peter 1:20–21:

> First of all you must understand this, that no prophecy of scripture is a matter of one's own interpretation, because no prophecy ever came by human will, but men and women moved by the Holy Spirit spoke from God.

These verses are some of the most challenging passages to understand and accept. Today it seems hard to find Spirit-filled men and women who preach the Word with authority. We have become skeptical of preachers and their messages. We dwell on the inconsistencies in what we hear and see from preachers and teachers.

Instead, as we journey in faith, we would do well to study the Word in small groups, listening to one another, and discerning how the Spirit is filling each of us, while also opening our hearts and minds to the truth of the Word of God. Through this learning together, our faith grows. It is this faith that comforts and protects us. This faith gives us confidence in what we say and do in the name of Jesus.

In this chapter, Peter briefly discussed the characteristics of those who identified themselves as followers of Christ. He reminded his followers of the promise of eternal life if they indeed followed the way Jesus has offered them. However, Peter also emphasized the rewards in this present life of doing good deeds as we serve others and attend to their needs. Peter continued to emphasize his credentials as a disciple of Jesus and as an eyewitness to the events that occurred during Jesus' ministry. And finally, Peter reminded his followers that only one empowered by the Holy Spirit was worthy of being trusted as a teacher of the Word of God. The power of the Word comes from the Holy Spirit through men and women who present themselves to embrace a life following the Spirit's direction.

Further Consideration and Action

Before moving on to the discussion and questions that follow, stop to consider the content of what you have just read. Peter packs elements of every one of his five major themes into this chapter. He does this intentionally because he is aware that his time with these folks and, in fact, his time in ministry is ending. He knows what is ahead of him as he confronts those who wish to silence his voice. One can sense his desperation in finishing the content of these two letters before he is no longer able to correspond with the churches and the people who have come to have faith in his teaching and his life example.

The faith offered to the Gentiles in Peter's time is the faith offered to present-day seekers. This faith is based on the teachings and ministry of Jesus Christ and his love and subsequent sacrifice for all people. This faith is the first step of the journey upon which many decide to travel. It is the basis for a quest for the Good News of Jesus Christ.

- Because of new believers being invited into faith communities, Jesus' message can be offered to a broader audience. How can you and I be a part of Jesus' ministry, inviting folks to hear and discuss the Good News? How can present believers communicate the urgency of the message for which Peter was willing to die?
- Who bears the responsibility for communicating the truth of the scriptures to those today who suffer in mind, body, or spirit?
- What part do you and I carry in teaching and living our lives as examples of experiences directed and informed by the Good News of Jesus?
- How do our words speak truth and encouragement?

Peter greeted his audiences with the phrase "grace and peace." In that phrase, he was offering a basis for friendship and hospitality among believers in Jesus Christ.

- When offering others grace and peace, what are the gifts you offer?
- What is grace, what is peace, and in whose name are those gifts offered?
- In other words, how can you or your church sincerely welcome people to your community of believers, a community that genuinely will love and support them, a group that learns together and worships together in thanks and praise?
- What do you hope the result would be in people's lives if we all lived in "grace and peace"?

Additionally, the journey of faith is a lifelong pursuit. It begins with accepting Jesus as Savior and continues to develop as we learn to understand the positive effects of the gifts Jesus offers all people. Some have called this journey a journey of righteous living. Living a life of righteousness and seeking to understand Jesus' gifts to all people begins to free followers from sinful natures. In this freedom, our lives are transformed. Just as those in the early church, through their example of faithful living and becoming credible witnesses of Jesus' ministry, we are also role models for Christian living. The strength of this collective witness, along with the power of the Holy Spirit, was how and why the early church grew so rapidly. Living a life of righteousness also implies that one is making room in their lives for the working of the Holy Spirit.

- What does that phrase, a journey of righteous living, mean to you?
- How might you describe how the Holy Spirit is at work in your life and in the life of your church?

2 Peter 1 spends a good deal of time emphasizing the importance of living by Christ-like standards, the fruits of the Spirit. We read in 2 Peter 1:4–9 about the virtues Peter is recommending. While personally meaningful, these virtues find their real impact on followers of Christ as they interact with one another. Just as significantly, these virtues impact how Christians relate to those outside the community of believers. The early church grew because it reached out to those who had never heard of Jesus, who never knew another way of living.

- A necessary part of being a Christian is to love all people enough to invite them into a caring fellowship in Jesus' name? How do you and your church set about accomplishing this mission?

There is a phrase used in many churches, "We can love others because God first loved us."

- Do you believe this? How would you describe your response to living according to that phrase?
- Based on the current climate in our world, how can we get across the message that knowing God loved us first empowers us to love others in return?

People are drawn to Jesus, and they grow closer to him by formal education, study, and direct experience of Jesus at work in their lives. Followers of Jesus pray for guidance, they worship Jesus, and they seek to repent of their former lives in favor of a new life in Christ. People who choose this path are the guardians, the messengers of the Gospel from generation to generation. If they accept Jesus' sacrifice and the Holy Spirit's power, they can acquire a faith others can see, in which others can believe, and in which they can have trust.

- How in your life have you gained more knowledge concerning the scriptures and what is required of you to speak with authority?
- How has the church prepared you for this critical task?
- How do you develop confidence in the words you speak on behalf of the Gospel?

Finally, one of the primary reasons false teachers arose is that people began to doubt the return of Jesus. The false teachers and prophets grabbed hold of that doubt. Their appeal to some was based on the seeming inconsistency of prophecy that Jesus was expected to return in their lifetime. He hadn't returned. Many false teachers thought that if this prophecy could be proved untrue, there might be other prophecies taught by Peter on which they could also cast doubt. False teachers and prophets were eager and willing to exploit the doubts of the followers of Christ.

- What did Peter say followers should look for in the words and teachings of people professing to have a differing interpretation of scripture?
- Why would false teachers betray the hope of understanding the scriptures by teaching false doctrine?
- Develop a strategy that you and your fellow church members might use to discover the truth of the information and the teaching you receive. Consider how you can confidently believe those who claim to know and preach the truth about scripture, its meaning, and application.

Chapter Eight

False Teachers and Final Judgment

G RAB YOUR JOURNAL for notes, then read 2 Peter 2:1–22 in the Holy
Bible before diving into this chapter.

> Let us pray:
> Gracious God, we believe in your words to us. We trust our
> lives to your care. Continue to protect us from those false
> teachers and prophets who would lead us astray. Help us
> discern the work of the Holy Spirit in the words and behav-
> iors of all who offer to instruct us concerning the scriptures.
> May we continue to grow in our knowledge of your Son,
> Jesus Christ, who brought to life the truth you would have
> us follow. We pray all this in the name of your Son, Jesus,
> the savior of our lives. Amen.

While driving home from church after worship, did you ever yell out
loud at other drivers who were speeding, darting in and out of traffic lanes,
and putting others at risk with their bad driving? And yet somehow you did
not imitate their behavior?

After leaving your weekly church service, did you ever notice members of the church gathering in the parking lot? Sadly, you know that some of those folks may have been criticizing the pastor or complaining about those "strange new people" in attendance. And yet somehow you welcomed the pastor's challenging message, and you were overjoyed to see new people visiting the church.

Did you ever hear folks who call themselves Christians spread gossip, rumors, lies, and hate-filled speech to describe those different from them? And yet somehow you prayed for understanding as you planned ways in which to welcome and love those that held opinions differing from yours.

Did you ever feel a particular sorrow for pastors and other church leaders who preached against all manner of sin and then were arrested themselves for adultery, abuse, embezzling, or some other sinful, hurtful behavior? And yet you asked God to pour down His mercy on those pastors and their actions? You asked God to help you remain firm in your faith even as those chosen to lead you were found to have misused your trust in them and their teaching.

What convinced you that your faith was strong enough to resist these detractors? Why didn't you turn your back on your faith? Why did you choose to continue to seek out people to help you discern the meaning and guidance of God's words found in scripture? Why have you remained faithful despite all the crazy, seemingly contradictory things that occur in churches?

Careful Discernment

From the very beginning, faith communities included those who spread false doctrine and misleading interpretation of scripture. These folks believed they heard in the scripture's message, opinions which permitted them to act in very contradictory ways from what others preached or believed. Some of these folks even attempted to convince others within their hearing that scriptures could have many interpretations. They suggested scripture was only a guide or conversation starter to discover on one's own what God really would allow in His name. Peter warned against these false teachers in this letter to his followers.

In 2 Peter 2:1, Peter began his letter, "But false prophets also arose among the people, just as there will be false teachers among you, who will secretly bring in destructive opinions." He added in 2 Peter 2:3, "And in their greed, they will exploit you with deceptive words." For the most part, these false teachers had no authority to preach or to be believed. They offered false dreams and false hopes to people desperately trying to find someone to follow. These false teachers were content with how they lived. They saw no need to change. They created interpretations of scripture, justifying and permitting diverse lifestyles. They also encouraged acceptance of a less demanding, less holy lifestyle than what is expected of followers of Jesus.

Peter denounced false teachers and prophets. Like other true prophets and teachers, Peter was a witness to the truthfulness and authenticity of his teaching as directed by God through the action of the Holy Spirit. In God's time, Peter warned that there would be a judgment against these false teachers for spreading their distortions. Peter sought to assure his followers that in the meantime God would protect them. In 2 Peter 2:9 we read, "Then the Lord knows how to rescue the godly from trial, and to keep unrighteous ones under punishment until the day of judgment."

Many of these false prophets, by outward appearance and behavior, seemed respectable and knowledgeable. Their words held just enough truth to gain the interest of those whose commitment to Christ wavered. Of course, false teachers sought to attract the same people Peter was trying to reach.

You and I know that change is challenging for folks. People are always ready to stay with what they know. This is what the false teachers understood. It was apparent; life following Jesus resulted in ongoing trouble for believers and their dealings with religious and civil leaders. The more determined false teachers heightened the tensions between Christ's followers and church and state leaders. They blamed Jesus' words for creating problems that never existed before his arrival among the people. Those teachers of false doctrine asked the crowds these questions: Is this where scripture leads followers of Christ, to be at constant odds with civil and religious leaders? What good was following Jesus if it just led to persecution and life in jail? Why not live as they always had—free from trouble with the authorities?

Many Jews and Gentiles were deceived by the slick words and interpretation of the scriptures offered by those spreading false doctrine. Given that, many people were attracted to these false teachers. Peter warned that for their misinterpretation of the scriptures, those false teachers would receive God's judgment.

In 2 Peter 2:10b–22, Peter is straightforward and unforgiving in his characterization of those false teachers, their person, and their message. One might wonder then why judgment for these false teachers was withheld until a future time. If their lifestyle and teaching were causing non-believers to distance themselves from Jesus' teachings, why were they permitted to keep preaching heresy and false interpretations?

The answer to this question is that God gives His people free will in choosing the conduct of their lives. While that's true, there is a more persuasive answer. That answer is based on how and why followers of Christ resist and counter false teaching even to this day.

The Kingdoms of Heaven and Earth

Two kingdoms affect our lives. God rules the kingdom of heaven, along with Jesus, the Holy Spirit, and all the other heavenly inhabitants. It is a kingdom of harmony and peace, love, and compassion. It is the kingdom for which we pray, "Thy kingdom come, thy will be done, on earth as it is in heaven." (Matthew 6:10). In part, we come to our faith in Jesus to be saved and made ready for the promise of eternal life in God's kingdom.

The second kingdom is the kingdom of this earth. To this kingdom, we are born. This kingdom is where we live. For good or evil, this kingdom is governed by powerful authorities who exercise their control over matters of state and matters of faith. This kingdom teaches believers and non-believers that they have free will to choose the direction of their lives. This kingdom is where false teachers and false prophets vie for the souls of those who inhabit the kingdom of earth.

As Christ's followers, believers have chosen to respond to Christ's sacrifice on their behalf by "imitating" Christ's behaviors, attitudes, and understandings. In that quest to be more like Christ, to find a faith that leads to salvation, Christians gladly support and serve the least, the last, and the lost. By choosing to live by Christ-like principles found in the kingdom of heaven, Christians straddle the two realms.

Which kingdom do they choose? The choices Christians make begin when they are baptized. They promise to live in a particular way for a particular purpose—to glorify God and His Son. Believers strive to impact folks' lives now, here on earth, while also working to prepare all believers for eternal life in heaven.

The choices believers make are in response to how they understand and experience what Jesus offers them through his life, death, and resurrection. The Great Commission of Jesus to his followers is to go into all the world, baptizing in Jesus' name and preaching the Good News to all people. Followers of Christ are expected to make disciples for Jesus, to transform the lives of suffering people, and to offer all humanity an alternative life of service and sacrifice for the Good News of Jesus. Believers are taught to use their testimony, witness, behavior, and outreach to save folks trapped for eternity by the teachings and directives of false teachers and prophets who battle for lives in this earthly kingdom.

God does not interfere in the kingdom of the earth. God has left life in the kingdom of earth to the concern and conduct of its occupants. For Christians, how they behave toward others on earth is their way of returning thanks for God's greatest gift, his Son. The task Christians are given prepares them for the promise and reward of salvation and eternal life. This task of relieving suffering and showing compassion to all people is the responsibility and commitment Christians undertake when they accept Jesus as their Lord and Savior.

And pursuing this mission is where hope begins, with new life in Christ, and where joy abounds as believers find new purpose and new commitment as they journey in faith. God's promises of salvation and eternal life are freely given to faithful believers. Living in those promises is a reason for many to endure the suffering and sacrifice followers of Jesus accept.

As individuals and as members of faith communities, Christians could not adequately complete their tasks without the Holy Spirit's power and presence working in their lives and their churches. Remember until Pentecost, when the Holy Spirit descended on those assembled, no one's teaching or preaching or attempts to heal in Jesus' name were successful. It wasn't until the power of the Holy Spirit entered into the lives of followers of Christ that their tasks would bear fruit as new members were welcomed into the community.

The Spirit also works to contain the efforts of false teachers and false prophets. It is by the Spirit that believers find the means and methods to contradict false teaching. To allow false teaching to win the day is to jeopardize the immortal souls of those who risk the judgment awaiting those who do not accept Jesus into their lives.

On hearing the Good News of Jesus Christ, potential followers have a choice to make. Will they accept Jesus into their lives and live by Christ-like standards and behaviors, or will they continue to live "in darkness"? The scriptures lead individuals to an understanding of the demands and responsibilities of living as Christ lived. Scripture identifies a way of life, an invitation to the Christian life, a life full of risk and reward, suffering, and happiness.

Once individuals have heard the Good News and have been offered the opportunity to accept Jesus into their lives, there are consequences for rejecting that offer. As Peter taught in 2 Peter 2:21, written with the false prophets in mind, "For it would have been better for them never to have known the way of righteousness than, after knowing it, to turn back from the holy commandment that was passed on to them."

To Peter, false teachers and false prophets were a genuine and ever-present threat to his followers' eternal souls. As brothers and sisters in Christ, followers of Christ are commanded to affirm, nurture, protect, and guide all those under their care. Christians are to show others a path that leads to salvation and eternal life in the kingdom of heaven. Christians are called to counter false teaching and false doctrine by living exemplary Christ-centered lives, in their thoughts, words, deeds, and service to those in need.

The difficulty, then and now, for followers of Christ is to learn who to trust for one's education while we study the scriptures. This is where prayer comes in. You and I are invited to talk with God, Jesus, and the Holy Spirit as we discern through our prayers the lessons found in scripture. Then as we interact with others in study, worship, and mission work, it is up to us to uncover the truth we hear and live by. As a United Methodist, I am guided by John Wesley's three general rules: do no harm, do all the good you can, and stay true to God's direction in your life. These three rules can guide us, regardless of our denomination, as we journey in faith toward answers to our most pressing questions.

Further Consideration and Action

Before continuing, take a moment to consider what you understand to be the responsibilities and duties of a Christian. From baptism, believers are encouraged to learn it means to live out the Great Commandment (Matthew 22:35–40) and the Great Commission (Matthew 28:16–20). The life of a Christian is one of discipleship and one that offers compassion and care to those in need. As you review the questions that follow, think about how you and those in your church or small group live out the expectations for Christlike living and ministry.

False prophets and teachers preach misleading lessons and deceive the people with their versions of scriptural interpretation. Their authority to preach and teach is not God-given or Spirit-filled.

- As followers of God's Word, how do we respond to the threat false teachers represent?
- What's our responsibility for countering their false teaching?

Peter tells us that God is always protecting God's people.

- In your life, how have you experienced God's protection from false teaching and false prophecy?
- How will ultimate judgment come to those spreading incorrect and hurtful interpretations of God's Word?

In 2 Peter 2:12–20, Peter vividly describes the characteristics and behaviors of false teachers.

- How would you recognize false teaching?
- How might the study of the Holy Bible be helpful to you?

- What standards do you use as you choose your teachers, pastors, and the church you will attend?

Remember at the first Pentecost, while Jesus' disciples were waiting for him to arrive, they were not able to preach or teach or perform miracles. It wasn't until the Holy Spirit settled on them that they were empowered by the Spirit to continue the ministry they had learned while traveling with Jesus.

The presence of the Holy Spirit gave the disciples the authority to communicate the Good News in ways that made their teaching and their actions worthy of trust. Those who were not empowered by the Holy Spirit relied on their own scheming to draw crowds. In the end, those who were touched by the Holy Spirit were believed as they ministered in the name of Jesus Christ. Even today, through the power and process of ordination, messengers of the Gospel receive the authority of the Holy Spirit and vow to do all they do in the name of, and for the sake of, Jesus Christ. It is important to discover the Holy Spirit at work in those who are your preachers and teachers.

- How do individuals and communities of faith invite the Holy Spirit into their presence to provide insight to those who seek to be protected from false teaching?
- How is the power of the Holy Spirit seen in the lives of present-day Christians and their churches?
- When you have questions of faith or questions about the Bible, who do you talk to? How do you discern if those folks are empowered by the Holy Spirit with the authority to speak on behalf of Jesus Christ?
- How might you go about finding a trustworthy teacher or pastor to help guide you on your lifelong journey of faith?

Chapter Nine

While We Wait,
We Do Not Lose Faith

BEFORE STUDYING THIS chapter, grab your journal and your Bible, and please read 2 Peter 3:1–18.

> Let's begin in prayer:
> O Creator God, while we wait for the return of your Son Jesus, let us not cease our efforts to find truth in our lives and the lives of those close to us. Help us see each other as a brother or sister in Christ while never neglecting or forgetting those who have yet to hear the Good News your Son offers to all people. Help us learn to live in peace and with respect and compassion for one another. Bring us and this world a new sense of unity. Prepare us to be authentic representatives of the Good News of your Son, Jesus Christ. We ask this in Jesus' name, the one who came in peace, the one who will come again. Amen.

I began this book by discussing the lost art of letter writing. I mentioned the letters I received from my father while he was a chaplain in the Army. Through those letters, I gained an understanding of people and places I never visited, and an appreciation for people and places entirely unknown to me. His encouragement to study what was new to me resulted in a lifelong desire to research and explore new insights as I seek to understand the needs of people and places and various lifestyles.

As I read these two letters written some two thousand years ago by the apostle Peter, I renewed my appreciation and commitment for what my faith requires of me today. I am called to be a living witness to my faith in my prayers, my presence, the use of my God-given gifts and talents, and in my service to all people.

Each day when I turn on the news or scan social media, I am amazed by the certainty folks believe they possess concerning a particular point of view about some contentious subject. From politics to social justice issues, conflicting opinions result in inequality, injustice, or unequal opportunity. People are still persecuting others in attempts to control and coerce behaviors and attitudes.

Several years ago, the answer for many Christians was found on a plastic bracelet inscribed with the initials WWJD, prompting us to ask ourselves, "What Would Jesus Do?" Those bracelets and that question have all but disappeared from our consideration. But the question lingers for followers of Christ. Amid all the information and misinformation, the news, and the fake news, what would Jesus do? What will we do while waiting to see what will change when Jesus returns?

I believe Jesus would trust his faith. Jesus would see beyond the present because he knows how all this confusion will resolve itself. Followers of Christ rely on faith in Jesus to find their reassurance, to give them a reason to hope and find joy in the present. We, too, know how it all ends. Jesus and the kingdom of God will be victorious. As you and I read Peter's letters, we are reminded Peter taught followers of Christ to trust the same quiet confidence Jesus possessed—trust and belief in God and God's steadfast love for us. Our faith promises that followers of Jesus will receive the rewards promised by God at our end. In the meantime, while we wait, faithful followers can know peace and purpose in this life. Keep this in mind as we complete the reading of Peter's second letter.

The Second Coming of Jesus

Central to many believers who lived during the early days of Christianity was the absolute belief that Jesus would return to earth during their lifetime. As folks began to die and new converts came to believe in Christ, the question of Jesus' return was seized upon by false teachers and prophets who used this seemingly scriptural inconsistency to sow doubt on the interpretation of all scripture. Peter addressed this in 2 Peter 3:3–4:

> First of all you must understand this, that in the last days scoffers will come, scoffing and indulging their own lusts and saying, "Where is the promise of his coming? For ever since our ancestors died, all things continue as they were from the beginning of creation!"

The false teachers purposely misinterpreted time and space issues to cast doubt on Jesus' return. They also used the confusion around scriptural interpretation to bring doubt on the integrity of Peter's teaching. Peter spent a good deal of time explaining how false teachers purposely encouraged folks to doubt scripture. He spoke of "God's time," where one day is like a thousand years. Earthly timekeeping methods weren't sufficient to identify the timing of Jesus' return. Peter also addressed the problem of knowing how long it had been since God began creating heaven and earth.

What did the false teachers have to gain by preaching their own views and interpretation of scripture? A life following Jesus was a life of righteous living. Life in Jesus made it necessary for individuals to give up old habits, old customs, and old behaviors. Many people resisted the changes Jesus required of his followers. Jesus upset the balance of power and privilege of many civil and religious leaders. He also preached ultimate judgment for living under the sinful practices of the day. If false teachers could convince others that life before Jesus was okay, Jesus' commands and attitudes might not prevail. Let me repeat 2 Peter 3:3-4:

> First of all you must understand this, that in the last days
> scoffers will come, scoffing and indulging their own lusts and
> saying, "Where is the promise of his coming? For ever since
> our ancestors died, all things continue as they were from the
> beginning of creation!"

False teachers made their point, especially to confused folks who were afraid because of what they experienced as followers of Christ, being so harshly treated by civil and religious leaders for their faith and belief in Jesus. They hadn't experienced or understood the joy in suffering or sacrificing for the Good News.

People could always revert to old habits and customs, living as they did before this "troublemaker" Jesus came on the scene. The false teachers were persuasive and took advantage of the anxiety that arose from following the demands of a life defined by Jesus' teachings.

Who would win the hearts and minds of the people? It came down to this: choosing the heavenly kingdom of God and Jesus for the benefit of all people, or the earthly kingdom ruled by powerful men and religious leaders for their own purposes.

Scripture held the answer. God and Jesus would win the battle. Unless the false teachers could offer a competing and believable interpretation of scripture, God and Jesus would indeed prevail, just as scripture promised. The Word of God stands firm against all attacks. Do you believe this? Do you see why the false teachers and the civil and religious leaders had so much to lose?

> In 2 Peter 3:11–12, Peter asked:
> Since all these things are to be dissolved in this way, what
> sort of persons ought you to be in leading lives of holiness
> and godliness, waiting for and hastening the coming of the
> day of God?

In some respects, this was a rhetorical question since these new converts to Christ had already pledged their lives to him to be holy and God-like in all their words, actions, and behaviors. Peter strived to assure those who believed in Christ that following Christ's example was how all believers ought to act while awaiting Christ's return. With their competing scriptural interpretations, the false teachers worked overtime to cast doubt on Peter's words and his authority to speak for God.

Peter presented one last appeal for faithfully waiting for Jesus' return. He said, "But, in accordance with his promise, we wait for new heavens and a new earth, where righteousness is at home." (2 Peter 3:13) The new heaven of which Peter spoke was the eternal home for all those who had lived by faith in Jesus. This heaven and the believers' places in it were God's promise to those who had lived and suffered for the sake of righteousness. The new kingdom on earth of which Peter spoke was heaven brought down to earth at the time of Jesus' return. Life on earth would mirror life in heaven.

The final section of this letter brought to conclusion all that Peter had preached about faithful living. Determined teachers of false doctrine continued to plot and scheme to alter scripture's meaning to cast doubt on Peter's witness and authority to speak on God's behalf. They did not prevail.

Peter recognized the temptations that were offered to the followers of Jesus. He knew the scriptures could be challenging to comprehend and even more challenging to follow. He encouraged followers to dive into the meaning of scripture to discover the demands and rewards of a life following Christ. Peter counseled followers to seek out teachers guided by the Holy Spirit. Peter continued to warn of false teachers who would use all sorts of distractions to cast doubt on the promises of God's Word.

Peter eventually had to depart from his followers. As he left them, he offered this benediction: "But grow in the grace and knowledge of our Lord and Savior, Jesus Christ. To him be the glory both now and to the day of eternity. Amen." (2 Peter 3:18)

And that is my prayer for you too. I hope as you studied Peter's two letters, you began to sense his success in finding the joy in his reasons to suffer, reasons to endure all the challenges of living as a follower of Jesus. He found joy in sacrificing and suffering as he offered the Good News of Jesus to all who would listen. Peter's journey of faith led him to live by Christ-like standards and behaviors. He willingly took on the suffering for faith that Christ knew. I hope Peter's teaching and the example of his faith journey inspire your own life-long journey in faith. I hope you discover the Good News of Jesus Christ and find your reasons for accepting and enduring suffering for the sake of your belief and faith in Jesus.

Further Consideration and Action

Through the study of Peter's two letters, we have had a glimpse of Peter's journey of faith. His faith was strong throughout because of his direct relationship with Jesus and Jesus' ministry. Those experiences convinced Peter to trust in Jesus and to be willing to sacrifice all for the sake of passing along the promise of salvation and eternal life that is offered to followers of Jesus.

Peter could not rest until he taught as many people as he was able about life following the Good News of Jesus. His joy, even in suffering, was due to his faith in the work he had been called to do. Peter, in turn, called all people to discover Jesus and to believe and have faith in a life following Jesus' example. Peter, through scripture, invites you and me to our own journeys of faith, of study, of sharing the Good News of Jesus. How will you and I respond?

Some believe that God may have postponed Christ's return to earth until all people had a chance to hear of a way to be saved by faith in Jesus. God understood the influence of evil in the world. God, in His love for us, patiently waits until we are ready to accept God's invitation to a new life following Christ. There are consequences for living an unrighteous and ungodly life, especially after you and I have been offered the choice to live according to Christ-like virtues.

- Do you believe this?
- What is your responsibility as a Christian to invite others to hear this message of salvation?

You and I are not to take our spiritual life for granted. We are regularly tested by the world, our friends, and family members to re-examine our need to be vigilant and steadfast in our faith. We are on a lifelong journey of faith, a journey that brings new insight and new challenges.

- What will it take for you to willingly accept this task?

What are the next steps you might take to further your study of scripture and to share your knowledge and insight with others who, because of you, may decide to accept Jesus as their Savior?

Remember the words of the old familiar hymn, "They will know we are Christians by our love."

- What in Peter's two letters has convinced you to follow a path of love and service in the name of Jesus and for the glory of God?
- How will loving others be a part of your faith journey? In what ways will you show your love for Jesus and for the people you meet?
- Peter found that teaching others about Jesus brought him joy even in times of spiritual suffering. This was his reason for enduring all the hardships in his life. Through this study, what reasons have you found that will comfort you as you endure suffering while in the service of Jesus and the Good News?

Chapter Ten

Reflecting on the Journey from Doubt to Faith

TWO ITEMS ARE essential to review as we come to the end of this study guide. First, I suggest reviewing the five general themes we find in Peter's two letters. Second, we ought to be clear about the answer to the question that began this study—why do people of God suffer?

The first general theme we looked at was **Belief in Christ**. That theme comes from 1 Peter 3:14b–16a.

> Do not fear what they fear, and do not be intimidated, but in your hearts sanctify Christ as Lord. Always be ready to make your defense to anyone who demands from you an accounting for the hope that is in you; yet do it with gentleness and reverence.

A central part of our faith journey ought to point to our being clear about what we believe concerning our faith in God, Jesus, and the Holy Spirit. Let's strive to connect our beliefs as Christians to living out our purpose and mission to do God's will. All this can be done with gentleness and reverence, trusting that our task is to plant the seeds of a desire to learn more about Jesus and the Good News he brings to all people. And then, trusting in the Holy Spirit to inspire others to seek Christ, continuing our never-ending journey toward a life ultimately directed by our faith.

The second general theme was **Suffering and Faith**. This theme is seen in two scriptures: 1 Peter 2:19–21 and 1 Peter 4:19. In the first scripture, we read:

> For it is a credit to you if, being aware of God you endure pain while suffering unjustly. If you endure when you are beaten for doing wrong, what credit is that? But if you endure when you do right and suffer for it, you have God's approval. For to this you have been called because Christ also suffered for you, leaving you an example, so that you should follow in his steps.

Whenever our actions or our beliefs make others uncomfortable, the possibility exists that those offended will confront us or try to silence us. We saw how often Peter and his disciples were either forced out of town, were thrown in jail, or eventually, were put to death for the discomfort they caused in some who heard the prophet's teachings. Yet Peter did not stop spreading his message of salvation and faith through Jesus. And for that firm belief, Peter suffered.

In the scripture we just read, if we endure suffering when we are right and suffer at the hands of those who disagree with us as we do the will of God, God will not leave us. God will stand with us in our suffering. Christ suffered for us. He left us an example of how we should respond to the suffering of those who seek to silence our voices.

In 1 Peter 4:19, we are guided by these words: "Therefore, let those suffering in accordance with God's will entrust themselves to a faithful Creator, while continuing to do good."

The motive of the false teachers we read about in Peter's letters was to turn us away from God and back to our former lives. Believers are encouraged by false teachers to give in, to stop our suffering, and to deny our faith in the protection and promises of God and God's Son. Peter reminded us that when we are acting according to God's will and finding resistance from those who disagree with us, we should continue by spreading the Good News and living by the example Peter demonstrated in his life and ministry.

The third theme that guided our reading was **Don't Be Discouraged or Misled**. This theme can be found in 2 Peter 2:1,3.

> But false prophets also arose among the people, just as there will be false teachers among you, who will secretly bring in destructive opinions. They will even deny the Master who bought them—bringing swift destruction on themselves ... And in their greed they will exploit you with deceptive words. Their condemnation, pronounced against them long ago, has not been idle, and their destruction is not asleep.

Since the serpent first spoke in the Garden of Eden, there have been false prophets or teachers who, for various reasons, have attempted to cast doubt on the Word of God and on believers who live according to God's commandments.

The question arises, why doesn't God just get rid of those false prophets? Several times in the New Testament scripture, we are told that believers will face trials and temptations so that the genuineness of their faith is made known to others. We need to test our faith and the strength of our belief in God, Jesus, and the Holy Spirit. God offers us that opportunity by not immediately removing those from us who challenge our faith.

God knows how it all ends. God has promised eternal life, salvation, and God's presence and grace to those who faithfully and obediently follow the scriptures. God leaves the choice up to us. It is the genuineness of our faith, a faith that we struggle to learn about and live by, that defines our life and our relationship with God and Jesus. The joy in living is to overcome all the temptations and distractions put in our way and to surrender our lives to do the will of God. This decision has to be ours. False teachers show us another way. But the choice is ours alone.

So we are to be on guard until the time when we reach a point on our faith journey when we stop listening to false prophecy and temptation. We stop measuring the impact and purpose of our lives by selfish standards. We dedicate all that we are, say, and do to furthering the Good News of Jesus Christ. As Jesus said in the Garden of Gethsemane, "Yet, not my will, but yours be done." (Luke 22:42)

In that simple sentence, we understand the joy and suffering expected of us as we go about our lives as obedient servants of the Word of God. Together as members of a community of believers, we can negate the messages false teachers try to spread. Our actions do speak louder than words to folks watching us as they observe the genuineness of our faith.

The fourth theme running through the two letters is **Receive Power from God**. Two scriptures shed light on what this theme can teach you and me: 1 Peter 5:10 and 1 Peter 3:18–22.

In the first scripture, 1 Peter 5:10, we read: "And after you have suffered for a little while, the God of all grace, who has called you to his eternal glory in Christ, will himself restore, support, strengthen, and establish you."

God and the prophets promised you and me at least two things: 1) God will provide all that is needed to survive the suffering brought on by others, and 2) faithful followers of Jesus will find eternal life in Christ. The first scripture tries to answer another of the big questions on the minds of those early converts to Christianity—the question of when Christ would return.

Jesus was expected to return while Peter and other prophets were alive. Despite everyone waiting for several years, there was still no indication when Christ would return and lead people to a better life. You will remember the timing of Christ's return was one of the points that the false prophets used to cast doubt on Peter's teaching. Another scripture, 2 Peter 3:9, adds, "The Lord is not slow about his promise, as some think of slowness, but is patient with you, not wanting any to perish, but all to come to repentance."

The second scripture, 1 Peter 3:18–22, describes the three days before Jesus rose from the dead on Easter morning. So that all might have a chance to know Jesus and be saved, Jesus spent time with those who had died before he had lived, and at that time, he offered them salvation by faith. He came to save them. He offered them a chance to repent of their lives and to find new life in Christ so that they might have eternal life. They heard the Gospel, and they had an opportunity to follow Jesus into eternity.

God delayed the Second Coming of Christ until all people had a chance to repent and receive salvation by faith in Christ. The timing of Jesus' return did cast doubt for some on the truth of Peter's teaching. But the delay in Christ's return is an act of mercy by God to make sure all people have a chance to hear the Good News of Jesus Christ and repent before final judgment comes upon humankind.

Peter prayed the people would stay strong in their faith and allow God and the Spirit to offer them the strength they needed to endure the suffering heaped on followers of Peter and Jesus. Peter's faith allowed him to trust and believe that God would make it all work. In Peter's faith, God would protect the people from false teaching. Peter trusted that God would straighten the winding and crooked path as folks began their journeys of faith.

The fifth theme, **Our Joy and Reward**, is based on 1 Peter 1:13 and 1 Peter 1:22. In 1 Peter 1:13, we read: "Therefore prepare your minds for action; discipline yourselves; set all your hope on the grace that Jesus Christ will bring you when he is revealed."

And in 1 Peter 1:22, we hear Peter directing believers: "Now that you have purified your souls by your obedience to the truth so that you have genuine mutual love, love one another deeply from the heart."

Peter was intent on his mission to offer the Good News of Jesus to as many people as he possibly could. In his own life, he had found hope and joy in the knowledge that God's love—God's grace—was offered to all. He also knew it was hope that gave people the will to move forward in their lives. Through baptism, followers of Jesus were freed from their sin and empowered by the Holy Spirit to live as Christ had hoped. As Christ found joy and satisfaction in his ministry and its effect on others, so too could his followers also find that same joy and happiness.

Jesus commanded folks to love one another even as God had loved them. Sharing that love with one's neighbors was central to Jesus' ministry. Peter directed his followers to offer their very lives in service to others. And as a reward for faithful obedience to that task, believers were promised new life here on earth and into eternity.

A key phrase is "when He (Jesus) is revealed." When one accepts Jesus as Lord and dedicates one's life to following Jesus' example, in a real sense, Jesus is revealed in and through the actions and words new converts now understand. When Jesus is revealed, followers can see and experience the life-changing forces of hope and love. All the struggles of faithful obedience to Christ seem to fall away and are replaced by joy in living as a disciple of Jesus.

Peter grew from a young fisherman to the Rock upon which Jesus built his church. Peter struggled with his faith, with his obedience, with his doubts. But in the end, he found joy and peace, even in suffering, for his witness and faith. This same joy and peace are offered to you and me by the same Jesus Christ who led Peter to new life. This is the joy and reward for our faithful obedience. This is a reason to embrace suffering without fear.

Final Words

Finally, let's return to the question asked in the introduction of this study. Why does God allow us to suffer?

Remember, we defined suffering in this way: "an act of giving up something valued for the sake of something else regarded as more important or worthy." God gave up his Son for something God believed was more important—in this case, to show God's love to all people. Jesus gave up his life so that you and I could be freed from the power of sin and freed from the fear of death. Suffering, it seems, is a result of sacrificing something one values to accomplish a greater purpose.

God doesn't allow us to suffer. God does not cause us to suffer. You and I accept our suffering in the sacrifices we make as we find our faith and live according to the example of Jesus. No matter how graciously offered, any sacrifice results in some degree of suffering, just as our definition of suffering suggests. We sacrifice something of value; we choose to suffer, knowing full well joy will be found in our suffering and sacrifice. We choose suffering just as Christ chose suffering so that others might discover blessing through our actions on their behalf.

There are four scriptures in Peter's first letter that shed light on why you and I would willingly choose to suffer for our faithful obedience. The first scripture is 1 Peter 2:19–20.

> For it is a credit to you if, being aware of God, you endure pain while suffering unjustly. If you endure when you are beaten for doing wrong, what credit is that? But if you endure when you do right and suffer for it, you have God's approval.

The key is knowing your sacrifices and your suffering are a result of doing what is right in the eyes of God. Peter had a message to preach. That message and prophecy upset many folks, so much so that he was chased from the towns and cities he visited. Eventually, he was put to death for confronting civil and religious leaders with inconvenient truth. The truth of Jesus' message preached by Peter threatened many who could not bear it under the scrutiny and demands of that teaching and example.

As Peter saw lives changing because of the example of Jesus, he sensed God's blessing and approval. Peter could endure because he saw how lives were being changed through newfound faith in Jesus. He could endure because he was doing what was right in God's sight. He was following not his will, but God's will.

The second scripture to review is 1 Peter 3:14: "But even if you do suffer for doing what is right, you are blessed. Do not fear what they fear, and do not be intimidated."

One of the hesitations some folks had in the early church was being identified as a follower of Jesus. They were afraid they would be thrown in jail or otherwise persecuted. The false teachers and religious leaders of that time spread confusing and contradictory doctrine. Those same teachers and leaders threatened folks who strayed from traditional customs and beliefs. But Peter reassured reluctant believers that they had nothing to fear from the threats and suffering brought on by others. God's blessing would protect and sustain faithful and obedient followers of Christ's teaching, just as Peter had preached.

The third scripture for us to consider is found in 1 Peter 3:17: "For it is better to suffer for doing good, if suffering should be God's will, than to suffer for doing evil." There is no reason to suffer or sacrifice something of value if the outcome is harmful to others. The reason to sacrifice or suffer for our faith is to be a witness to the joy found in remaining faithful to Jesus and his teaching no matter what befalls us. Peter reminded his audience that knowing what one believed was an essential component of why one would willingly suffer in the first place. Suffering to further the will of God always results in God's approval and blessing. Suffering so that others might see Jesus at work through our sacrifices is a holy way to live.

Finally, we read in 1 Peter 4:19: "Therefore, let those suffering in accordance with God's will entrust themselves to a faithful Creator, while continuing to do good." Trusting God with our lives and surrendering our lives to God is one result we find as you and I journey in our understanding of our faith. Trusting in God's love, protection, and God's overall care for us, brings you and me peace and confidence. That makes us strong enough to endure suffering, misrepresentation, and disapproval from those challenged by our witness to the Word of God and the teaching of Jesus Christ.

Peter calls us to continue to do good. He calls us to be faithful followers of Jesus. He calls us to give our lives to doing the will of God. This most certainly will result in some suffering and sacrifice, but the joy of helping others to meet Christ in their lives is a great reason to endure and continue to be a visible sign of faithful living. Do you believe this?

Let me share one last scripture with you as a benediction of sorts as we come to the end of this study. Peter said:

> Finally, all of you, have unity of spirit, sympathy, love for one another, a tender heart, and a humble mind. Do not repay evil for evil or abuse for abuse; but, on the contrary, repay with a blessing. It is for this that you were called—that you might inherit a blessing.
>
> 1 Peter 3:8–9

Never be overly concerned by suffering or sacrifice as you share the Good News of Jesus Christ with folks who need a kind word or an invitation to a new way of living. Let the peace of Christ and God's love be the path that leads you to discover your reasons for suffering. May the joy you find on your journey of faith comfort you, protect you, and give you confidence even as you are called to endure, suffer, and sacrifice just as Peter did, just as Jesus did. Amen.

About the Author

An experienced teacher, coach, administrator, speaker, and for the last 20 years an ordained Elder in the United Methodist Church, Jonathan has been active in formal and informal ministry settings. His education includes a B.A. in Government, an M.A. in counseling, an MBA in Marketing, and an M.Div. in Theology. He has counseled both individuals and families who are actively involved in examining their lifelong journeys of faith. Jonathan's teaching is based on practical, everyday lessons derived from how scripture, experience, tradition, and reason help individuals to encounter faith. He writes for those who consider themselves people of faith as well as for those who are seeking new spiritual knowledge.

Love this book? Don't forget to leave a review!

Every review matters, and it matters *a lot*!

Head over to Amazon or wherever you purchased this book to leave an honest review for me.

Thanks very much

Made in the USA
Monee, IL
09 June 2021

70653861R00069